ScheckEats

Cooking Smarter

Friendly Recipes with a Side of Science

Jeremy Scheck

HARVEST

An Imprint of WILLIAM MORROW

HarperCollins books may be purchased for educational, business, or sales promotional use. For information, please email the Special Markets Department at SPsales@harpercollins.com.

FIRST EDITION

Designed by Melissa Lotfy
Food photography copyright © 2023 by Jeremy Scheck
Portrait photography pages x and 220 copyright © 2023 by Lexi Brown
Illustrations copyright © 2023 by Nancy Swire Arons
Food styling by Samantha Seneviratne, Laura Manzano, and Fatima Khamise
Prop styling by Anne Eastman
Lined backgrounds © cepera/Shutterstock

Library of Congress Cataloging-in-Publication Data has been applied for.

ISBN 978-0-06-326558-5

23 24 25 26 27   TC   10 9 8 7 6 5 4 3 2 1

To my brothers—Leo, Gabriel, and Evan, who all desperately need my help in the kitchen and could benefit from reading a book—and to our sister, who likely can't read this because she's a dog.

Setting the Table

of Contents

Welcome

Some people save lives; I make avocado toast. I have always read cookbooks from cover to cover like novels. I've been hooked on them ever since I found old editions of *The New York Times Cookbook* and *Mastering the Art of French Cooking* in the one-dollar bin at my school's used book fair. Even in high school, the rainbow of Barefoot Contessa spines filled my bedroom bookshelf.

In my early teens, I taught myself to cook by reading all those scavenged books and watching instructional videos online. I would then experiment every day in the kitchen and bring goodies into school for my friends to taste. I always found recipes more interesting when they included explanations rooted in food science. It's much easier to remember techniques if you actually understand why they work—otherwise, they just sound like an arbitrary order of operations!

The process of writing a cookbook is slow. It takes two *years* from signing with a publisher for the book to actually get to the shelves, and that was three years *after* I had the concept.

My self-teaching and researching prepared me to work at a bakery and start a food blog in high school. These experiences then led me to teach cooking classes at Williams-Sonoma, and take more than a dozen college classes in food science, culinary arts, agricultural science, and nutrition.

The process of writing a cookbook is slow. It takes two *years* from signing with a publisher for the book to actually get to the shelves, and that was three years *after* I had the concept. I had the idea for this book in 2018, during my freshman year of college. At that point, I had maintained a little food blog for three years. My grandma Karen was probably the only one really reading those early recipes, but it was satisfying enough for me just to see all my favorite recipes put in one place, like a virtual cookbook of my own. At that time, I was already eager to write a proper cookbook, so I reached out to Jenn Segal, a cookbook author I admired, who graciously agreed to take a call from me. She told me something to the effect of, *"It's a great idea, but it's nearly impossible to get published as an unknown."* She advised it was probably best to focus on growing the blog. Even though I was disappointed by the reality check, knowing what I know now, her advice was 100 percent spot-on. Even if you have the best idea ever, it can be extremely difficult to get a book agent's attention, let alone a publisher's. After our conversation, I made a few tweaks to the theme of my blog, but mostly I just sat on the idea.

A year and a half later, in March 2020, my friends and I were sent home from college as the Covid pandemic took force. With only a few days' notice, I had to pack up my first college apartment, without knowing if I'd ever be back. Like many others, I turned to TikTok to find some escape from the chaos unfolding around me. I started my channel, making recipes with the random ingredients

I had to use up in my pantry before I left school—everything had to go! To my surprise, the videos actually garnered views, likes, and comments.

Although working in a professional bakery improved my chops, I still consider myself first and foremost a home cook, and I never *ever* call myself a chef, which is a title you really need to earn. To give myself some credit, I do think I'm pretty good at cooking, but mostly because of my interest and curiosity. I spend an extraordinary amount of time reading about food, trying new things, and learning about the science of cooking . . . but I don't think I'm ever going to be a Dominique Crenn or a Thomas Keller. If I had to guess, I'd say my particular aptitude lies in communication before anything else. If I have one talent, I like to think it's my ability to explain anything I've learned—whether it's to a five-year-old, a twenty-year-old, or an expert in that field. I discovered this at Williams-Sonoma, first when I taught some baking demonstrations as a high schooler (pics on page 187), then later when I was hired as an employee to teach their weekly classes. Every week my boss would hand me a recipe from corporate and tell me I was teaching it the next day! Sometimes I had to teach a recipe I had never made before, so I had to go home and practice until I was comfortable. Even though I was often a little in over my head, I always managed to rise to the occasion and learned so much in the process. I explained recipes to kids as well as adults fifty years my senior. I always held their attention, and I'd like to think they walked away with at least one new tip or technique.

As my TikTok videos gained momentum, it was exciting for sure, but I was also a college student—a sophomore at Cornell University. Getting my degree and having a full college experience was still a high priority for me. Eventually, as the Covid landscape shifted, I returned to campus as a junior, continuing with TikTok and Instagram videos while reimmersing myself in college life.

Since attending a Spanish-immersion elementary school, I've had a lifelong interest in foreign language. I learned to read, write, and do math in Spanish before English, despite speaking English at home. Having my first five years of grade school in Spanish keeps it ingrained in me. Even better, it was a public magnet school—gratis.

In between high school and college, I lived with a family in Spain and worked as an au pair. At Cornell, I majored in Spanish and Italian, which deepened my interest in the related European and Latin American cuisines. It's a unique privilege to study another culture in the context of their own language using primary sources. In addition to my language courses, I took an equal number of food-related courses.

In one of my food science classes, we had to design our own ice cream flavor—and make fifty gallons of it. In an animal science class, we traveled throughout Northern Italy to learn about dairy farming and cheese production. (Though the academic portion of the course focused on dairy farming and economics, I weaseled my way into that class because of my Italian major.) I desperately wanted to learn about it all—everyone else in the class was either an animal science or agricultural science major. The majority of the other students came from dairy-farming families, so the class was a neat way to compare Italian and American farming practices. I also took horticulture and viticulture classes, pruning grape vines in Cornell's teaching vineyard and learning how wine was made. Since it was for "education," we got to taste wines in class, even though we were underage. On the last day of one of my horticulture classes, our professor, Dr. Marvin Pritts, a berry expert, took us to his house and made us a meal of venison from a deer he had hunted. In one of my nutrition courses, we cooked new recipes every week and had to design our own menus on a SNAP budget that still met all our nutritional requirements. Even though my college experience had its ups and downs between the pandemic and some health issues I dealt with, I still felt like I won the lottery with the number of spectacular classes I was able to take.

As my online presence grew, people started taking me more seriously, which was hilarious because I am a profoundly unserious person. (After all, I nearly named this book *Cooker? I Just Met Her!* just because I like the pun.) TikTok and Instagram allowed me to reach people all over the world, and talking about food gave us all a break during such a turbulent time. Finally, all the moving parts seemed to be aligning for this book to take shape.

About This Book

I am a no-BS kind of guy, so I will tell you my exact goals for this book:

1. **Revamp Classics**—a fresh take can make your favorite dishes more accessible and more delicious.
2. **Share Everyday Winners**—these recipes are tried and true, and grounded in staple ingredients. No need to shop for ten different things each time you want to make a new recipe.
3. **Be the New Guide**—I may come from Gen Z, but this book is for all ages, from curious kids to busy parents, empty-nesters and single adults. No experience? No problem. Decades of experience? I bet I can still pique your interest.

I rarely set out to reinvent the wheel when I am cooking. If we're being honest, there aren't a lot of genuinely new recipes being invented. **Big Cookbook probably doesn't want me to say it, but 99 percent of the time, we're making our own version of an already existing concept**. I have trouble with the pretense of claiming that I created all these recipes out of thin air, and it's frankly not what I set out to do. I am not the first person to make crispy potatoes or vodka pasta, and I sure as heck won't be the last. If I can't be the genius who originally figured it all out, I might as well focus on how best to explain these recipes instead. It surprises many people to learn that you can't copyright a list of ingredients. Maybe that's why KFC and Coca-Cola guard their formulas so tightly. That said, you could give one hundred people the same ingredients and still get one hundred slightly different outcomes. The only part of a recipe you can truly (and legally) claim for yourself are the directions! I always find this fact a bit astonishing, but also a bit sweet because the method is where you can add a personal touch. You'll find this book is filled with tried-and-true recipes, sprinkled with nuggets of food-science tips, and peppered with occasional unexpected twists and turns.

I aim to strike a balance with my recipes—easy enough for a first-timer and still engaging enough for the more experienced cook. I made the recipes in this book more accessible by limiting the number of extraneous ingredients and streamlining the equipment required. I didn't want anyone to have to search high and low for a laundry list of rare ingredients or to spend hundreds of dollars on a sous vide system. Many recipes draw only from my list of staple ingredients, which is on page xv, and the recipes that focus on a specific protein or vegetable are still heavily grounded in those staples, which I always keep on hand.

You'll find this book is filled with tried-and-true recipes, sprinkled with nuggets of food-science tips, and peppered with occasional unexpected twists and turns.

I won't ask anyone to stock up on unnecessary impulse-buy gadgets, but I will point out when it's worth investing in a multipurpose item such as a decent blender, which is good not only for smoothies but also soups, vinaigrettes, and pesto. I prefer simple, multiuse kitchen tools, like a good chef's knife, tongs, and a Microplane.

Sometimes, I find that recipes muddle the technique behind them; even when you follow them perfectly, it can be a challenge to understand the steps along the way. It's like following a GPS in the car, then realizing you have no idea how you arrived at the destination. Whether it's a cherished family recipe, something I learned from another cook, or something I came up with on my own, I try to convey recipes in a clear format that not only guarantees success, but also hopefully teaches something new along the way.

The recipes I've included in this book sometimes cover similar ground or feature the same essential principles with varied ingredients or flavors, but this is on purpose—it helps to highlight the underlying technique. For example, you might first make crispy roast potatoes, and later try the crispy sweet potatoes, too, noticing and appreciating the similarities and differences.

I hope the pages of this book become dog-eared and spattered with everyday use. The takeaway from making each one of my roast chicken recipes should be how to roast a chicken, rather than the ingredients of one specific recipe. **That way, when you're stranded on a desert island, you'll be able to figure it out over an open fire. Or something like that.**

—Buen provecho, buon appetito
and bon appétit!

Staple Ingredients

At a Glance

Staple ingredients are the ones I always have on hand, no matter what. If I run out, they need to be replaced. I consider other ingredients, like certain veggies and all proteins, "star ingredients," since I stock them based on what looks good at the store, what's on sale, and what's in season. About one-third of my recipes can be made using only staple ingredients, and the rest are made with just a few star ingredients added. In this book, star ingredients are underlined in yellow, so you can see at a glance what staples you may already have on hand and what star ingredients you may need to pick up.

The list that follows is a starting point, not an end point.

This list is not meant to limit you in any way. It is based on what I personally buy for my own kitchen, but everyone is entitled to their own likes and dislikes. **Don't like spicy foods?** Leave out the Calabrian chili bomba paste, red pepper flakes, and chili powder. **Vegan?** Use veggie stock and ditch the dairy section. Some people will look at ten spices and wonder how on earth they will ever use them all; meanwhile others will feel that the ten I chose barely scratch the surface of their daily use. **Please feel empowered to tweak the list to your personal taste and food culture.**

✳ All the illustrations were hand-painted by my grandma Nan

Oils

Good extra-virgin olive oil
Neutral oil (such as peanut or avocado)
Toasted sesame oil

Vinegars

Apple cider vinegar
Balsamic vinegar
Unseasoned rice wine vinegar

Flavorful Liquids

Chicken stock
Soy sauce
Wine

Cans

Canned beans
Canned whole tomatoes
Coconut milk (not light)

White Powders + Dry Goods

Diamond Crystal kosher salt
  (see page 22 for a note on seasoning)
Potato starch
All-purpose flour
Panko bread crumbs
Baking powder
Baking soda
Granulated sugar
Brown sugar
Dried pasta
Rolled oats
Rice
Nuts
Dates
Dried cranberries

Condiments

Calabrian chili bomba paste
Dijon mustard
Maple syrup
Sweet chili sauce
Pomegranate molasses
Apricot jam
Honey
White miso
Tomato paste
Chicken or beef bouillon paste

Dairy + Eggs*

Heavy cream
Crème fraîche (or sour cream)
Whole milk Greek yogurt
Whole milk
Butter
Large eggs
Parmigiano Reggiano
Cream cheese
Pecorino Romano

Seasonings

Herbes de Provence
Black pepper
Dried oregano
Szeged sweet paprika
Ground cumin
Za'atar
Garlic powder
Ground cinnamon
Red pepper flakes
Sesame seeds

* Eggs are not dairy LOL

Plants

Garlic
Fresh ginger
Bird's eye chili, also called Thai chili
Cilantro
Celery
Jalapeño
Shallots
Onions
Potatoes
Carrots
Lemons
Limes
Parsley
Rosemary

Baking-Specific Extras

Semisweet chocolate
Powdered sugar
Vanilla extract (I use homemade; see my
    recipe on page 178)
Rainbow sprinkles

This list is designed to mirror my shopping habits.

When I head to the grocery store, I have two broad categories of foods in my mind: staples and stars. **Staple Ingredients** are the ones from this list. These are my dependable, tried-and-true workhorses. Star Ingredients are fresh, seasonal fruits, vegetables, and proteins. On a typical food-shopping day, I replenish whatever staples I am running low on, then choose two or three star produce items and two or three star proteins. Some people like to go in with a concrete plan in mind. Personally, I like to see what looks good, and then choose star ingredients based on what inspires me in the moment.

Staples in Depth

Because the staple ingredients are so important to the book, I wanted to dedicate some space to briefly talk about each one. They are listed here in alphabetical order. I am including a few brand names based on what I use in my own kitchen, because it may help you find the exact item. If you're starting with a bare cupboard, my list might seem like a lot. And even if you cook frequently, you might see a handful of items or brands you don't typically stock. But having an arsenal of good-quality ingredients always on hand means that even the simplest meal is going to taste amazing.

- **All-purpose flour:** Such as King Arthur brand. Your go-to for baking, dredging meats, and roux making.

- **Apple cider vinegar:** It adds a friendly brightness to braises and vinaigrettes without an overbearing pungency. I buy the generic brand.

- **Apricot jam:** Such as Bonne Maman. A flavorful way to add sweetness to a dish; melts into sauces. Make a vinaigrette inside a near-empty jar, or just make a PB and J.

- **Baking powder:** Such as Rumford. It's a mix of baking soda plus a powdered acid and cornstarch, so it does not require another acidic ingredient in the recipe to create lift.

- **Baking soda:** Such as Arm & Hammer brand. An alkaline leavener indispensable for baking, it's three to four times more concentrated than baking powder. Usually used in combination with an acid in a recipe, such as lemon, yogurt, buttermilk, or vinegar. You can also keep a box in the fridge to reduce odors.

- **Balsamic vinegar:** Did you know it's made from grapes? For salad dressings, marinades, sauces, or drizzling over cooked vegetables. Top-quality balsamic vinegar is aged twelve-plus years and is very sweet and very expensive—you don't need that kind for daily use.

- **Bird's eye chili or Thai chili:** Roughly ten times hotter than a jalapeño but less hot than a habanero or Scotch bonnet. I like to use it in stir-fries and sauces.

- **Black pepper:** I use it in almost every savory dish. Never *ever* use preground pepper; it tastes like sawdust (and a shaker is no more convenient than a grinder).

- **Brown sugar:** The molasses inside adds nuance and moisture in baking. Not just for baking, also good in spice rubs!

- **Butter:** There is no substitute for real butter. My go-to is Kerrygold unsalted, but any European-style butter is recommended. American-style butter tends to have 1 to 5 percent more water in it compared to European. Many European butters are salted and cultured, and while they may speak more languages than us, I mean "cultured" in the fermented yogurty way . . . While cultured salted butter is delicious on bread, I use unsalted butter for most things in the kitchen. You can always add salt, but you can't remove it if it's already there. Many people don't know that butter is extremely low in lactose, containing only trace amounts, meaning lactose-intolerant people who are not allergic to other chemicals in dairy usually tolerate butter with no issues. Store extra in the freezer.

- **Calabrian chili bomba paste:** This is probably the most niche ingredient on the list, but they have it at Trader Joe's, and it's easily purchased online. It's spicy, a bit sour, and a little funky. *Great* in salad dressing and sauces.

- **Canned beans:** I usually have at least chickpeas and black beans on hand. One thing to note is the texture can vary by brand; Trader Joe's chickpeas, for example, tend to be firmer (less cooked).

- **Canned whole San Marzano tomatoes:** Unless it's tomato season, canned tomatoes will be more reliable than fresh at the grocery store. They are picked and preserved at their peak ripeness.

- **Carrots:** Versatile, sweet, hardy, cheap. They stay good in the fridge for a long time, but you can prolong their freshness even more by cutting as desired and storing in a jar of water in the fridge.

- **Celery:** Carrots' best friend. Even next to each other alphabetically! While large sticks of it raw do not appeal to me, a fine mince of raw celery adds so much freshness to something like an egg salad. It's also essential in mirepoix and soffritto—at the base of many dishes.

- **Chicken or beef bouillon paste:** Such as Organic Better Than Bouillon. Extremely useful in a pinch, offers very concentrated flavor, and keeps in the fridge for a long time. They make a vegan version too.

- **Chicken stock:** For soups and sauces and stews. Sub veggie if need be. Can be skipped if using a good quality bouillon paste.

- **Cilantro:** Parsley's evil twin (at least, for those who don't like the taste—it's a genetic trait . . . but I can't live without it).

- **Coconut milk (full-fat):** For stews, some baking, and many Southeast Asian and Caribbean dishes.

- **Cream cheese:** Such as Philadelphia. Not just for bagels. Can be mixed into savory sauces, used as the base of dips or fillings, or made into frosting. Store extra in the freezer.

- **Crème fraîche:** Sour cream's richer cousin. Great dolloped on top of potatoes or soup, or swirled into sauces.

- **Dates:** A natural sweetener, great whole or chopped into little bites. I tend to buy ones on the smaller side if I am cooking with them and not eating them plain. Soak them in water for 10 to 15 minutes, drain, blend with a couple teaspoons of water, and add salt for a caramel-like sauce free of refined sugar.

- **Diamond Crystal kosher salt:** For everything except whipped cream. It's very important to remember that the relative intensity of a salt depends on the density of the variety and brand (see page 22 for more). Morton kosher salt tends to taste about twice as salty as Diamond Crystal because it's denser; if you are substituting Morton, use half as much as my recipes call for. I recommend avoiding iodized salt; it's not doing your food any favors.

- **Dijon mustard:** Emulsifies vinaigrettes, adds complex flavor to other dishes. Even if you *think* you don't like it, it is worth putting a little bit in your salad dressing!

- **Dried cranberries:** Good in salads, baked goods, and on top of oatmeal. Can melt into braising liquid.

- **Dried oregano:** One of the only herbs I like better dried. Adds earthiness.

- **Dried pasta:** For best quality, look for bronze-die extruded and slowly dried pasta. My preferred grocery store brand is De Cecco, and for a premium option, I love Afeltra, but there are many good options, including Wegmans' Amore brand tagliatelle.

- **Eggs:** I buy large ones. Great on their own, necessary in most baking.

- **Fresh ginger:** Indispensable in Asian cuisines, also great in baked goods. Can be stored in the freezer to make it last longer (and it's easier to grate).

- **Fresh rosemary:** A woody herb, it has a better texture when it's cooked. There's nothing like it on chicken or potatoes.

- **Garlic:** Pungent when raw; sweet and mild when cooked. Use it in the base of a sauce, stuff a chicken with a whole head of it, or roast it.

- **Garlic powder:** Tastes different than fresh garlic, and adds intense cooked-garlic flavor to spice rubs and flour dredges.

- **Good extra-virgin olive oil:** Good olive oil is actually fresh-pressed olive juice, and it should be enjoyed and replenished frequently. Dark glass bottles help preserve freshness. It's very personal in terms of what varieties will be your favorites. Extra-virgin olive oil is my go-to oil for most European and Mediterranean dishes. Don't use it for everything, though; I find it tastes strange when paired with East Asian flavors. Pick something good enough to eat raw, but not terribly expensive.

- **Granulated sugar:** Such as Domino brand. A baking staple, but don't ignore its utility in balancing out savory dishes.

- **Ground cinnamon:** Versatile spice for a pop of warm sweetness.

- **Ground cumin:** For aromatic and nutty flavor. Good in many different cuisines. I use ground for most things, but whole can be especially good in South Asian dishes.

- **Heavy cream:** Makes for rich sauces and baked goods. I look for heavy cream without additional ingredients and, when possible, one that isn't ultra-pasteurized.

- **Herbes de Provence:** A French spice blend that includes thyme, rosemary, oregano, and marjoram. Sometimes it has lavender too. Can be sizzled in oil to awaken the flavor.

- **Honey:** A natural sweetener, can balance savory dishes or be used in baking as well. I look for raw, local varieties.

- **Jalapeño:** A vegetal spicy pepper on the milder side. Good sautéed and raw. Did you know chipotles are dried and smoked ripe jalapeños?

- **Lemons:** Bright, acidic, good in almost every Western cuisine. Bottled lemon juice is *never* a good substitute for the real thing. See page 194 for more on bottled juice.

- **Limes:** Irreplaceable in tropical cuisines. A squeeze of lime can be the finishing touch that makes an okay dish great. Bottled lime juice does not do the flavor justice. See page 194 for more on bottled juice.

- **Maple syrup:** I buy Grade A amber "rich taste" or Grade A dark "robust taste." Natural sweetener, good in copious amounts on top of pancakes, but also in baked goods and to balance acidity in salad dressings and sauces.

- **Neutral oil:** I prefer peanut or avocado oil. Good for high heat, frying, baking, and whenever flavorful oils like olive or sesame are not appropriate.

- **Nuts:** I usually keep three types on hand to use in recipes: slivered almonds, pine nuts, and candied walnuts.

- **Onion:** I usually have red and yellow on hand. Can be eaten raw or used as the base of infinite sauces and dishes. Cheap kitchen workhorse.

- **Panko bread crumbs:** Gets things crispy when you use it in a dredge! Can also be used inside black bean burgers (see page 108) or meatballs.

- **Parmigiano Reggiano:** Pure savory and umami flavor. A lactose-free cheese. Don't buy the pregrated. For everyday use, aged twenty-four months is good. Real Parmigiano Reggiano will say "Parmigiano Reggiano" exactly on the label or signage, and it will be stamped on the rind. Impostors may be labeled as "parmesan" or "Parmesan Reggiano." See page xxiv for more info.

- **Parsley:** Adds a fairly neutral freshness to a dish. One of my most used garnishes.

- **Pecorino Romano:** A sheep's milk cheese, a bit saltier and funkier than Parmigiano.

- **Pomegranate molasses:** Concentrated pomegranate juice popular in Persian and Middle Eastern cuisines. Sweet-and-sour flavor is great in marinades and salad dressings. Also just amazing mixed with extra-virgin olive oil as a bread dip. One of the few ingredients that might be challenging to find, but available online, at a store like Whole Foods, or your local Middle Eastern grocer. You can also make it yourself with pomegranate juice, sugar, and lemon juice.

Is Cheese Vegetarian?

Most traditional cheeses including Parmigiano Reggiano are made with animal rennet. Rennet is a mix of enzymes used to coagulate milk, allowing you to separate the curds and whey (like Little Miss Muffet). Curds are the solids that become the cheese itself, and whey is a protein-rich liquid byproduct of cheesemaking, which can be used to make ricotta and protein powders, and as an ingredient in animal feed.

Until 1990, almost all cheeses were made with animal rennet, which is extracted from the stomach lining of a young ruminant, such as a calf. Only a tiny amount is needed; the average 1 kg of cheese (2.2 lbs) contains 0.0003g of rennet enzymes.

In 1990, Pfizer introduced the first FDA-approved genetically modified food ingredient, fermentation-produced chymosin (FPC), a rennet that comes from fungus but is marketed as "vegetable rennet." Since then, most industrial cheesemaking has switched over to FPC because it is much cheaper than animal rennet. Nevertheless, many cheeses like Parmigiano Reggiano maintain traditional methods, and would lose certifications if they deviated.

Animal rennet is a bit of a gray area for some vegetarians, since it comes from enzymes inside a calf's stomach, but it's not literally *meat*. This gets philosophical really fast, and it comes down to how you define *vegetarian* and how you define *meat*.

For example, is being vegetarian not eating steak or not killing the cow? Unlike with veganism, which is an ethical ideology more than a diet alone (including prohibitions on non-food animal products such leather), I think *vegetarian* tends to refer more to diet alone.

It becomes more nuanced when you consider that rennet is extracted as a coproduct of veal (82 percent of global veal production occurs in Europe)[1], but calves are not killed specifically for the rennet.

At the end of the day, it's your choice to consume animal rennet or not, and there are definitely vegetarians who strictly avoid animal rennet, and there are plenty of vegetarians who do not care either way.

Most domestic imitations of Parmigiano Reggiano (labeled "parmesan" or "ParmeSAN Reggiano") are made with FPC and are widely accessible. They can taste just fine, but you didn't hear it from me (I want to be allowed back into Italy). Check the ingredients to be sure.

For the purposes of this book, recipes with cheese in them but no meat will be listed as vegetarian, along with other dairy products and eggs. Of course, if you are not comfortable with animal rennet, there are plenty of substitutes.

- **Potatoes:** I usually have some russets and some yellow potatoes on hand.

- **Potato starch:** Good for thickening sauces, or as a coating to get things crispy. You can substitute cornstarch if needed.

- **Red pepper flakes:** Offers a neutral heat.

- **Rice:** My personal favorite brand is Nishiki. I also usually stock jasmine and arborio rice. Different cuisines favor different varieties, and it is best to adjust accordingly.

- **Rolled oats:** For oatmeal and granola. Can be made into oat flour with a blender, and also good in crumble desserts.

- **Sesame seeds:** Add a pleasant nuttiness to Asian and Middle Eastern dishes, also great in baking.

- **Shallots:** Onion's garlicky cousin. A little sweeter and more flavorful.

- **Soy sauce:** Ubiquitous in East Asian recipes, but also a flavorful way to add salt in Western dishes. A couple teaspoons can go a long way in a sauce, stew, or marinade. You can also substitute a gluten-free tamari.

- **Sweet chili sauce:** Mostly sweet and a little spicy, it's a good shortcut condiment to keep in the fridge. Use it in marinades, sauces, or on its own.

- **Szeged sweet paprika:** My mom lived in Hungary for two years, where they take paprika very seriously. This is the best type that can be easily found at most US grocery stores.

- **Toasted sesame oil:** Aromatic, for use mostly in East Asian dishes. It has a fairly high smoke point, but is often best drizzled on as a finishing touch to a dish.

- **Tomato paste:** I like the type that comes in a toothpaste-style tube, so you can easily use a little at a time. Make sure to always cook it in oil for a few minutes before adding liquid.

- **Unseasoned rice wine vinegar:** For bright East Asian flavors.

- **White miso:** Adds salt and savoriness in marinades or swirled in sauces. Can also be used in baking. Some brands have gluten, some don't (gluten-free brands are usually labeled as such; otherwise assume it has gluten).

- **Whole milk:** For coffee, oatmeal, cereal, baking.

- **Whole milk Greek yogurt:** Such as FAGE brand. Season it and use as a chicken marinade, or use it in baking to add moisture and lightness.

- **Wine:** I keep at least one red and one dry white. These don't have to be expensive, but use something good enough to drink. No "cooking wine." Good for depth of flavor in sauces and for deglazing pans. For an alcohol-free substitute, use verjus.

- **Za'atar mix:** The word *za'atar* itself refers to a specific type of thyme-related herb, and the *mix* also called za'atar contains sesame seeds and sumac. It's great in marinades, on meat, and classically with bread and olive oil.

Protected Designation of Origin

When certain products have been made the same way for generations, governing bodies like the European Union often certify the products to protect from imitation or adulteration. You've probably heard that champagne can only be made in Champagne, France; otherwise it's just plain-old sparkling wine. This concept applies to many food products.

Terroir is a French word that refers to the unique characteristics that a specific region can impart to a food. It can encompass environmental factors like climate and human factors like farming practices.

The types of certified products include heritage animal breeds, cheeses, meats, or crop varietals. Some protected products you might have heard of include Prosciutto di Parma, San Marzano tomatoes (Pomodoro San Marzano dell'Agro Sarnese-Nocerino), Phú Quốc fish sauce, Kalamata olives, and Shetland Lamb.

"Protected designation of origin" (PDO) status denotes the strongest link to a terroir. The name and initialism changes depending on the country of origin—for example, in Italian, it becomes "denominazione di origine protteta" or "DOP" and in French, "Appellation d'origine protégée" or "AOP." (Just to confuse you even more, the most protected Italian wines are labeled "DOC" and "DOCG" and the French ones are "AOC," but these still fall under the umbrella of PDO.) If you are ever unsure what a legitimate label should look like, a quick internet search is worth it.

If a product is PDO certified, the producer can voluntarily use the special red and yellow badge, which is helpful for consumers for quick identification. The seal usually appears on signage or printed labels, but it is not necessary to be legit. For example, a factory cut wedge of Parmigiano Reggiano often will have the badge on its packaging, but a grocer who buys a whole wheel and cuts it up is probably not printing the badges for their plastic wrap.

So how do I know if my Parmigiano Reggiano is the real deal? (See page xxii for more about Parmigiano Reggiano.) The full name "Parmigiano Reggiano" is always spelled out completely on the label. Be careful! Sometimes knockoffs write "Parmesan Reggiano" or something that appears quite similar. The rind has the words "Parmigiano Reggiano" stamped all over it with dots. If you're just buying a chunk, you should see a fragment. If you can see the entire wheel, the letters "DOP" will also be on there. Commercial packaging or signage will display the red and yellow "DOP" badge.

Why does any of this matter?

I see PDO certification as analogous to organic certification. A product does not need to be certified to be good, but knowing there is some oversight gives some peace of mind. That said, I grew up getting milk and eggs from a local farm. The farm wasn't "organic certified," but in talking to the farmers, we learned that the certification process is very expensive, even though their farming practices exceeded organic standards.

Tools and Equipment

If you were moving into your first apartment or house and didn't have any cooking equipment, this is exactly what I'd recommend. It is not a very long list, but it's just about everything you need to make all the recipes in this book.

- **Balloon whisk:** For sauces, baking, and aerating dry ingredients without sifting.

- **Blender:** This is the only appliance I'm going to force you to use in this book besides your oven and stove. I think it's the best way to make salad dressings, and I also use it for pesto, soups, and smoothies. You can use a regular one for all purposes, or use an immersion blender, which works well for everything except smoothies. I really like a Nutribullet or an Oster on the budget side, but I use my Vitamix every day and have found it well worth the investment.

- **Box grater:** I mainly use this for larger amounts of coarsely grated cheese, and also for veggies like carrots and radishes.

- **Chef's knife:** You don't need to spend a fortune on it—you just need to keep it sharp. On the budget end, Mercer Culinary is great. I also like Misen, Five Two, Hedley & Bennett, and Zwilling.

- **Cutting board:** I really hope this is self-explanatory. But Fredericks & Mae makes the prettiest ones.

- **Danish dough whisk:** Replaces the need for a mixer in many instances. This is my most esoteric tool, but these whisks are very cheap and useful for so much. It's stiffer than a normal whisk but open enough that stuff doesn't get stuck in it. I've found it to be the best way to cream butter by hand for baking recipes, but you can also use it for things like mashed potatoes.

- **Measuring cups and spoons:** For liquid measuring cups, get a Pyrex (or similar glass measuring cup) with at least two-cup capacity. Remember, one cup of a dry measuring cup is not the same as one cup wet (due to density), so they are not interchangeable. Some measuring spoons come double sided, which can be nice so you don't have to clean them as much in the middle of a recipe.

- **Meat thermometer:** Optional but recommended. These are very inexpensive and take little space to store, but give you peace of mind not only from a foodborne-illness standpoint, but also a doneness one: you can measure the right temperature for medium rare, medium, and so on, to avoid the guessing game.

- **Microplane zester:** I use this in so many recipes, sweet and savory. Not only will it give you the finest Parmigiano Reggiano shavings, it'll also zest citrus, and you can even use it for whole nutmeg, garlic, and frozen ginger. I cook with a lot of citrus zest, either as a garnish for savories or in the batter for desserts, because it often has more flavor than the juice. Without a Microplane, it's really hard to get just the right amount of zest off the rind without getting into the bitter pith.

- **Serrated knife:** Same advice applies as for chef's knives. I use these for bread, tomatoes, chocolate, and nuts.

- **Silicone pastry brush:** This is one of those things that is really hard to substitute if you don't have one. It's useful for spreading marinades on meat, especially while they're cooking, and for egg wash when you are making certain baked goods. You can also find options with bristles more like a paintbrush, but I find the silicone ones easier to clean.

- **Silicone spatula:** For mixing, maneuvering, and flipping. I find the larger and sturdier, the better. I like Tovolo brand.

- **Tongs:** Useful for so many kitchen maneuvers. I prefer ones that are all metal or silicone tipped; just make sure they are heat-safe.

- **Vegetable peeler:** I leave the peels on most veggies unless it's absolutely necessary to remove them for a recipe (see more of my cooking philosophy on page xxxi). A lot of people like the Y-shaped peelers, but I find a regular OXO swivel peeler works great.

Cookware

I do not believe nonstick cookware is essential, and well-seasoned cast iron *is* nearly nonstick; see page 2 for more on that.

- **4-quart saucepan:** As the name suggests, good for sauces, but if you are cooking for just one or two people, you can usually get away with using this size for boiling pasta or making soup. You don't always need something huge. I recommend a stainless steel one from Calphalon, Made In, or All-Clad.

- **6-quart (or larger) dutch oven:** This is a workhorse for braises, soups, and stocks. You can definitely find affordable ones at stores like Marshalls or HomeGoods, but if you have the means to invest in a Staub or Le Creuset, you won't regret it.

- **8 × 8-inch baking dish:** It can be tempered glass, such as Pyrex, or metal. I recommend USA Pan. Good for cakes and things like mini lasagna.

- **9 × 13-inch baking dish:** It might seem like it's not that different than an 8 × 8-inch dish, but the surface area is almost double. For this size, I find ceramic or glass most useful for something like roasting a chicken, but you can also still use it for baking.

- **Half sheet pan (13 × 18-inch baking sheet):** One of the most versatile pieces of bakeware. You can roast vegetables and meat, or bake a dozen cookies on it. USA Pan makes my favorite.

- **Large, oven-safe skillet:** This can be stainless steel or cast iron. Calphalon makes a good budget option for stainless steel, and Lodge cast iron is very affordable. I also love Staub, Made In, and All-Clad if you're looking to invest.

Baking-Specific Items

- Kitchen scale

- Muffin tin

- Wire rack

Don't Poison Yourself
Food Safety 101

According to US government statistics, every year around 3,000 people die of foodborne illness and approximately 128,000 people are hospitalized. I don't share this to scare you, but I do think we should exercise a healthy amount of caution. I am ALL about having fun in the kitchen, but it's important to remember food safety. I'm sharing some of my best practices, but remember: **as scientists get new data, safety recommendations can change, so it is always best to check online when in doubt.** The website foodsafety.gov is a great resource to get the latest recommendations, and they always indicate when the information was last updated.

What Is Cross-Contamination and How Do I Avoid It?

In a nutshell, anything that touches raw meat, seafood, or eggs should be thoroughly cleaned before touching anything else—this includes cooking equipment, surfaces, and your hands. Cross-contamination happens when bacteria or other pathogens from these raw ingredients come into contact with other foods or utensils, which may not be heated or cleaned enough to kill bacteria.

For example: cutting up raw chicken, then using the same knife to cut vegetables without thoroughly washing it in between. If you have more than one, use different cutting boards and knives for prepping meats and vegetables.

By contrast, roasting a chicken with veggies in the same pan, provided they are all cooked to the proper temperature, is *not* cross-contamination, since all the foods are cooked enough to kill any potential bacteria.

How Do I Know if My Meat Is Cooked Enough?

Different meats have different temperatures at which they are safe to consume. You've probably seen a warning on every menu in the US that says something like: *Consuming raw or undercooked meats, poultry, seafood, shellfish, or eggs may increase your risk of foodborne illness . . .* This is to address the risk of not meeting the recommended temperatures.

The USDA provides guidance on safe internal temperatures for meats, and you can look them up online. *However, many people are surprised to learn that these temperatures aren't static.* For example, while 165°F is known as the temperature at which chicken is safe to eat, the breast meat can be a bit dry if cooked to that temperature. While 165°F is universally safe, 160°F can be safe if the temperature is held for at least sixteen seconds. If the temperature holds for three minutes, you can eat chicken that's cooked at 150°F. If you have a meat thermometer, you can use it to make sure that the temperature is safe.

How Do I Stay on Top of Outbreaks of Foodborne Illness?

In the United States, the CDC shares information on its social media and website whenever there is a major outbreak or food recall. Salmonella, listeria, *E. coli*, and norovirus (just to name a few) are no joke. Random food items get recalled all the time, from romaine lettuce in the Pacific Northwest to enoki mushrooms in Texas or chicken thighs in Vermont. Staying up to date could save a life, or at minimum a few days of unpleasant symptoms.

I Made Too Much Food! How Do I Save It for Later?

Store foods in the refrigerator or freezer in airtight containers, or well wrapped with plastic wrap. When reheating food, always reheat it until it's piping hot (bacteria love lukewarm environments).

Never leave perishable food (like leftovers) out of the fridge for more than two hours. It may be conventional wisdom to let leftovers cool completely before placing them in the fridge, but with twenty-first-century refrigerators, *this is not the best practice.* According to the USDA, warm foods can be placed in the refrigerator as long as they are not in huge containers. If you have a large pot of hot soup, for example, divide it into shallow containers before chilling. While you can let foods cool down within the safe two-hour window, it may be smarter to put them in sooner rather than later, so you don't accidentally leave them out too long.

How Long Can I Keep Food?

We all have that one friend or family member with an iron stomach. These are the people like my grandpa Michael, who can eat ten-day-old leftovers without a second thought. For most of us mortals, this is not advisable. I try to use leftovers in the fridge within three days. Most raw meats shouldn't stay in the fridge longer than one or two days, unless they are packed and sealed with an expiration date that says otherwise. For the most accurate recommendations on a case-by-case basis, see the Cold Food Storage Chart on foodsafety.gov.

If you buy too much meat or are planning to cook it later, freeze it right away, and then thaw overnight in the fridge when you want to use it. In addition, when stored correctly, some fruits and vegetables can last a long time in the fridge. Apples, carrots, celery . . . these are very durable!

Should I Wash My Meat Before Cooking?

This is a controversial topic, because many recipes and cultural practices will tell you to wash meat either with water or an acid like vinegar or lime juice. At the time of writing (2023), the CDC recommends *not* washing meats such as chicken, because it can spread germs like salmonella in your kitchen. They maintain that raw chicken is ready to cook out of the package. Should you choose to wash it anyway, the CDC offers some advice for minimizing the spread of germs.[2]

If you choose to wash chicken, do so as safely as possible:

1. Run the water gently over the chicken to reduce splashing.
2. Then immediately clean the sink and area around the sink with hot soapy water and sanitize them thoroughly.
3. Wash your hands for twenty seconds.

I do find it funny that the CDC tells us "no!" but also tells us how best to break their recommendation, since many people won't follow it anyway. These guidelines work as valuable harm-reduction.

Practice "First In, First Out"

I learned this phrase while working at a local bakery, and even though it might be common sense, I find it helpful to keep in mind. You should eat the oldest things first before getting to the newer stuff. This ensures that you have less waste and spoilage. If you want to get even more organized, keep a roll of masking tape and a Sharpie by the freezer and label everything with the date before storing it. In addition, if you're stocking up on things you already have (e.g., buying a new carton of milk before finishing the first), put the new item *behind* the older item to ensure you reach for the old one first.

Wash the Outside of Fruits and Vegetables . . . Even if You Don't Eat It

Okay, I'm not going to sit here and lie to your face and say that I always do this . . . but avocados, lemons, pineapple, melon: even though you might not eat the skin, it's advisable to wash the outside of these foods because when you cut them, the knife can bring with it whatever dirt/pesticides/fecal material is on the outside.

My Cooking Philosophy

1. **If I don't need to peel it, I don't.**
   I don't go out of my way to make extra
   work for myself. My mother always
   told me that the peels of a fruit or
   vegetable are the healthiest part. I
   might not have fact-checked this as
   a kid, but it is generally true that the
   peels contain lots of fiber, vitamins,
   and antioxidants. This is great news,
   but more importantly, *life is too short
   to spend all day peeling potatoes or
   apples or ginger or carrots.* Unless it's
   a food where the peel is actually not
   supposed to be eaten, I rarely find it
   worth peeling. Every once in a while,
   it can be worth it for presentation, but
   most times, just make sure you give the
   skins a good wash.

2. **I go for the real thing.** I am not a
   low-fat kind of person. I want real
   ice cream, not the diet stuff, full-fat
   yogurt, whole milk if I'm having it, and
   most importantly, real butter, not any
   imitation. I would rather eat a slightly
   smaller portion of the real thing than
   gorge myself on the diet version. This
   doesn't only apply to animal products.
   In fact, I try to eat about two-thirds of
   my meals plant-based. But when I'm
   having a meal with no meat, I'd much
   rather get my complete proteins from a
   dish like Cumin Stewed Chickpeas (see
   page 103) and rice as opposed to a meat

   substitute. Whatever you like is your
   business, but that's just me.

3. **I add flair where it counts.** This comes
   down to personal discretion, because
   we may value different things. For
   example, since I save so much time
   not peeling my potatoes, I have time to
   chop up some fresh herbs. Whereas I
   don't think peeling potatoes elevates
   them, herbs make almost everything
   better. They add flavor, freshness, and
   dimension to dishes, and I think they
   are often overlooked in home kitchens.
   Plus, I think chopping herbs is fun and
   peeling is not.

4. **I consider "taste" versus "flavor."** Even
   though we can experience thousands
   of unique flavors, most "flavor" is
   perceived through our olfactory sense
   (smell), *paired with* the five tastes in
   our mouth. There are actually *only*
   five tastes that our tongue can sense
   on its own: salty, sweet, bitter, sour,
   and umami (savoriness). All other
   complexities in flavor come from
   two types of smelling. The first (and
   obvious), sniffing with the nose on your
   face, is called "orthonasal olfaction" in
   scientific language.
   More importantly, your nose also
   gets aromas from the passageways
   inside your mouth as you chew,
   which is called "retronasal olfaction."

Retronasal olfaction is how most flavor is perceived.

It's easy to add lots of *flavors* to a dish with spices and herbs, but you also always need to account for the five main *tastes*. Not everything needs major contrast like "sweet and sour" or "bittersweet," but adding a *bit* of sweetness to a rich, salty, and savory dish or a touch of salt to dessert can really help round everything out and make it feel more balanced. A lot of times, when something doesn't taste great, it is just missing a pinch of salt or a squeeze of lemon or lime to wake it up.

8 Quick Tips

1. **Have lots of little tasting spoons.** As much as we'd like to cook everything perfectly by eye, the only way to know if you've really seasoned it right is by tasting things as you go.

2. **Salt at every stage.** Food tastes a lot worse when you salt it only at the dinner table. Adding a little at each step of the cooking process gives you a more balanced taste.

3. **Don't be scared of high heat.** Browned bits in cooking are flavor (see my explainer on the Maillard reaction on page 65). You can't get that if you're only using medium to low heat.

4. **Recognize which ingredients are there for structure, and which are just for flavor.** Experimenting can be really fun, but before you make any major changes, make sure to think through what ingredients are crucial to the dish and what can change without throwing everything else off. For example, in a cake recipe, you can make flavor adjustments, but you probably shouldn't mess with the flour or baking powder at first.

5. **If something is missing a "wow" factor, consider the five tastes** (see page xxxi). A dish can be flavorful and aromatic with lots of herbs and spices, but if you don't have a balance of salt, sweet, and sour (and to a lesser extent bitter and umami), it will probably taste flat. You might just need a pinch of something sweet, a touch of salt, or a squeeze of lime.

6. **Remember to "bloom" spices, tomato paste, and flour in savory dishes.** Spices, tomato paste, and flour all need to be cooked *before* adding any liquids to the pan. Once you add liquid (other than cooking oil), these won't cook in the same way. Awaken the flavor of dry spices by cooking them in butter or oil before adding anything wet to the mix. Tomato paste and flour (in sauces) taste off when they aren't first cooked in butter or oil—it gets rid of the gummy, raw edge.

7. **Get acquainted with your oven temperature.** You'd be surprised how common it is for ovens to run even as much as 90°F hotter or colder than shown on the temperature gauge. You don't have to be checking constantly, but it can be helpful to know if your oven runs hot or cold. Use an oven thermometer to check the actual temperature inside, and then adjust the setting accordingly. (More about oven temperature on page 114.)

8. **Preheat your pan before adding the oil.** Before adding oil or butter to a stainless steel pan, you should first let the pan sit over medium heat for 1 to 2 full minutes to really heat up. On a microscopic level, this makes the surface smoother and less prone to stickiness.

Housekeeping

On Dietary Labels

Throughout the book, I've labeled recipes as "vegan," "vegetarian," and "gluten-free," and I often give suggestions for substitutions. I hope that these notes are helpful and make my recipes more inclusive, but I also recognize that it is a little arbitrary where to draw the line with the suggestions. For example, I use soy sauce in a lot of recipes, and it is easy to substitute tamari to make it gluten-free. This is a swap I make all the time in my own kitchen, and it's hard to taste the difference.

However, if you make enough changes, you can make almost anything gluten-free or vegan. For the purposes of my book, it felt silly to note that the gluten-free option in a pasta recipe is to use gluten-free pasta . . . it's obvious. You can also use gluten-free bread in my tomato toast recipe, but I am not sure that merits its own note.

People who follow specific diets are usually their own best experts at making recipes work for them. I don't love gluten-free pasta or fake butter, so I don't include those as substitutions, but if you have dietary restrictions or just prefer those ingredients, you can use them, and you'll have an even wider breadth of recipes that fit within your own guidelines.

On Serving Sizes

I'm not a huge fan of prescribing serving sizes, mostly because they seem like wild guesses at best. My dad could eat four chicken thighs; meanwhile my mom would be happy with one. So how many people does a recipe of eight thighs serve? Two clones of my dad or eight clones of my mom. How much pasta you want depends on whether you're having it as a main dish or an appetizer. The yields I give in the recipes are meant as a loose guide. But everyone's appetite and serving style are different, so you should look at the amount of food called for in the ingredient lists and think about how much you and your friends and family might eat.

Can I Use an Air Fryer?

Short answer: Yes, any time one of my recipes recommends convection, you could use an air fryer instead.

Long answer: There is no such thing as "air frying." It's really just a small convection oven with *marketing*. These can be a great appliance for small spaces, and they preheat super quickly. I do not like air fryers when they are used to make things that are only good deep fried—I would never use one to make "healthy" Southern-style fried chicken or any other nonsense of that sort. But they are remarkable for skin-on chicken, fish, roast veggies, and reheating frozen food.

A Note About Salt

It's important to remember that different brands of salt have different densities, which affects how salty they taste. All the recipes in this book were tested using Diamond Crystal kosher salt. If you use another brand, you may need to adjust the quantity. A teaspoon of one salt brand can be a totally different amount than another. Occasionally, I use flaky salt such as Maldon as a finishing touch. Flaky salt adds visual appeal and texture, and is one of the least intense salt shapes, since it takes longer to break down in your mouth. While I love flaky salt, it's definitely a flourish and I don't think of it as a "required" staple ingredient. Wherever I suggest flaky salt, kosher salt is fine to use instead. See page 22 for more about this.

Breakfast

The most optional meal of the day

Nonstick Cookware

First of all, if you are happy with your current setup, that's what's important, and you don't need to change it. However, if you ask me, I generally do not recommend nonstick cookware. Instead, I prefer a well-seasoned cast-iron skillet, which is naturally resistant to sticking (see Cast-Iron Pans, page 24). I also like stainless steel cookware, and you can avoid making a sticky mess of it with proper use.

The two main reasons I do not recommend nonstick cookware are that:

1. high-heat cooking breaks down the coating;

2. it shouldn't be used with metal cooking utensils.

I do not like to fearmonger about "chemicals" broadly, since everything in the world is made up of chemicals, including me and you; however, there are also potential risks from nonstick coatings that are worth considering: Nonstick pans made before 2013 can contain perfluorooctanoic acid (PFOA), which is categorized as "possibly carcinogenic to humans" based on limited evidence in humans that it can cause testicular and kidney cancer, and limited evidence that it can cause cancer in lab animals."[3]

PFOA is also an environmental concern, since it's a pollutant in water that does not degrade naturally. Based on a publication in *Nature*, "hundreds of millions of people in Europe, the United States, Australia and China are still exposed to levels of these compounds that exceed what regulatory agencies deem healthy."[4]

Newer nonstick pans are usually coated with polytetrafluoroethylene (PTFE), also known as Teflon. While Teflon is *manufactured* with the same PFOA, it is not believed to migrate into food in any significant amount,[5] even when heated past recommended temperatures; however, Teflon cookware that gets too dry from being left on the heat too long can cause flu-like symptoms. Fumes from even normal use of Teflon, while deemed safe for humans, can cause sudden death in birds.[6] Always make sure to ventilate the kitchen well if cooking with Teflon, and do not use it if you have pet birds. "Ceramic" nonstick pans are actually made with a silicone-based coating (not real ceramic), and while they may be PTFE-free, in my experience, the nonstick coating wears off in a couple months if not weeks.

With everything considered, I think it is fine to have one or two nonstick pans—a large skillet or griddle—as long as you do not have pet birds, and you take care to:

1. Only use medium to low heat

2. Never use metal utensils

3. Store it without scratching

4. Reserve for extra-sticky foods like pancakes and eggs

How to Avoid a Sticky Mess with Stainless Steel

- **Preheat your pan.** Place your empty stainless steel pan over medium heat for 1 to 2 full minutes before adding any oil or butter. If you need to lower the temperature later, that's fine. Stainless steel has microscopic pores and gaps on the surface. When the metal is heated, the molecules expand, which smooths out the surface.[7] Generally 1 to 2 minutes is enough time, but if you are unsure if your pan is hot enough you can easily use a bit of water to test. Moisten your hand under the sink and flick some water droplets onto the pan. If they just sizzle away, it is not ready yet. The pan is ready when your water droplets instead stay rounded like little beads. This phenomenon is called the Leidenfrost effect. When the pan is hot enough, the water will create an insulating vapor layer around the droplet that keeps it from boiling away.

- **Don't skimp on the fat.** Make sure to use 1 to 2 tablespoons (at least) of oil or butter if you want to avoid sticking. When the pan is properly preheated, the fat will spread out better over the pan. I don't want to hear about the extra calories; it will be okay.

- **Heat the oil or butter before adding anything else.** Just like with the first step, you don't need to wait an eternity, but do give your fat at least a full 60 seconds to heat before adding any vegetables or meat.

- **Make cleanup easier.** If anything does stick, it can be helpful to let stainless steel pans soak in the sink for a few minutes . . . or a couple hours. If anything is really hard to get off, you can fill the pan with water, let it come to a boil, then simmer for a couple minutes. This is like soaking it on steroids and will help release any stubborn bits.

Crispy Fried Eggs in Calabrian Chili Butter

VEGETARIAN
DAIRY-FREE OPTION ... Use olive oil instead of butter
GLUTEN-FREE

ALL STAPLE INGREDIENTS

MAKES 1 SERVING

1 to 2 tablespoons unsalted butter

1 or 2 large eggs

1 teaspoon Calabrian chili bomba paste

Kosher salt and freshly ground black pepper to taste

I love a buttery fried egg in the morning, especially with hot sauce, and Calabrian bomba paste is the perfect way to add in that flavor to the cooking process, instead of using it as a topping.

1   Heat a skillet over medium heat for 2 minutes before doing anything else.

2   Add enough butter to generously coat your pan.

3   When the butter is bubbly and spread out, crack the egg(s) over the pan (I break them on the counter and open them over the pan).

4   Let the egg(s) cook over medium heat (do not touch them) until the edges start to become golden. Tilt the pan a little so the butter pools at the bottom and use a small spoon to baste the uncooked parts of the whites, avoiding the yolk. Stir the chili paste into the butter in the pan. The egg(s) will take a couple minutes to cook.

5   Season with salt and pepper. If you want the top cooked more, you can use a metal spatula to flip the egg(s) and cook for another minute or two. It can be helpful to slide the spatula under the yolk(s) before flipping to make sure they are loosened.

Leftover Veggie Omelet

MAKES 1 SERVING

VEGETARIAN OPTION ... Skip the meat in the filling
GLUTEN-FREE

2 large eggs

1 to 2 tablespoons unsalted butter, or more as needed

Filling of your choice (or omit):

I like about ½ cup leftover cooked vegetables, 2 tablespoons grated cheese, and 2 slices of cooked bacon cut into little pieces

Kosher salt and freshly ground black pepper to taste

Fresh herbs for garnish (optional)

Before the owners of Carriage House in Ithaca retired after my sophomore year of college, I loved getting brunch at their place. They always had a wonderful omelet, filled with seasonal veggies and a bit of cheese and bacon. Since the restaurant has closed, I now have to re-create it myself. If you have leftover roasted vegetables from dinner, this is a smart way to repurpose them.

This recipe is for one omelet, and you definitely need 1 to 2 tablespoons of butter at minimum to keep it from sticking, but if you decide to make multiple, you might only need a little bit more in between batches.

1   Crack the eggs into a bowl; beat with a fork until the yolk and the white are homogenous.

2   Heat a small skillet over medium-high heat for 2 minutes. Add the butter and heat until it gets foamy.

3   Reduce the heat to medium and pour in the eggs. Let sit until the edges start to cook.

4   Cover the pan with a heatproof plate or lid; reduce the heat to medium-low and cook until the top of the omelet is mostly cooked through, about 1 minute.

5   Add the filling and salt and pepper, and use a silicone spatula to fold the omelet in half.

6   Serve with fresh herbs if you have them.

Jammy Tomato Toast with Soft Scramble

VEGETARIAN
DAIRY-FREE OPTION ... Use all olive oil instead of butter

MAKES 1 SERVING

2 tablespoons extra-virgin olive oil

About 12 cherry tomatoes, halved

Kosher salt and freshly ground black pepper to taste

2 tablespoons Caramelized Onions (page 26)

1 big slice sourdough bread

2 tablespoons unsalted butter

2 large eggs, beaten well

This is something I like to make in the summer when the tomatoes are so good and you have so many that you don't even know what to do with them. I usually make this as a toast because I like how the tomatoes pair with sourdough, but you could also use them as an omelet filling (see my omelet recipe on page 7)!

If you do not want to make caramelized onions beforehand, you can also just sauté some onions in the olive oil for 5 to 6 minutes before adding in the tomatoes. It is not the same as sweet caramelized onions, but it will add lots of flavor in a fraction of the time.

1   Heat the olive oil in a large skillet over medium heat. Add the tomatoes. Season with salt and pepper and cook, stirring occasionally, until they really soften and start to break down, 5 to 6 minutes. Stir in the caramelized onions, and keep the tomato mixture over low heat while you make the eggs and toast.

2   Toast the sourdough while you start on the eggs. If you don't have a toaster, you can carefully toast the bread under the broiler or in a hot pan on the stovetop.

3   Heat a small skillet over medium heat for 1 minute before adding the butter. Let the butter sizzle, then add the beaten eggs. Stir nonstop with a silicone spatula, until the eggs are a tiny bit less cooked than you want them (the residual heat will continue to cook them a bit after you take the pan off the stove). Season with salt and pepper.

4   Put the eggs on top of the toast, then spoon the tomato mixture on top of the eggs.

Homemade Granola

MAKES ABOUT 4 CUPS

VEGAN OPTION ... Use maple syrup instead of honey
VEGETARIAN
DAIRY-FREE
GLUTEN-FREE ... (oats are naturally gluten-free but may be cross-contaminated if they are not certified)

2 cups rolled oats

2 large handfuls nuts of your choice

⅓ to ⅔ cup seeds, such as chia, flax, or sunflower

1 teaspoon kosher salt

1 teaspoon ground cinnamon or other seasonings of your choice

3 tablespoons coconut oil or neutral oil

¼ cup maple syrup or honey

Handful of dried fruit (optional; I like dried cranberries or blueberries)

Homemade granola is super easy to make, and it's cheaper than store-bought.

1 Preheat the oven to 300°F and line a half sheet pan with parchment paper (if desired, for easier cleanup). Combine the oats, nuts, seeds, salt, cinnamon, oil, and maple syrup. Spread the mixture out on the baking sheet. Bake for 1 hour, or until crunchy and deeply golden brown, stirring every 15 minutes or so.

2 Let cool completely, then stir in the dried fruit (if desired!).

3 You can store cooled granola in an airtight container for at least 2 weeks, or freeze it for up to a few months (let sit out overnight to thaw).

Smarter Tips

✳ Feel free to switch up the spices, types of nuts, and seasonings.

✳ If you like your granola more clumpy, don't spread it out as much on the baking sheet.

Apple Streusel Muffins

MAKES 18 MUFFINS

For the batter

12 tablespoons (1½ sticks/170g) unsalted butter

1 cup (226ml) good-quality maple syrup

⅔ cup (150g) whole milk Greek yogurt

2 large eggs

1 teaspoon vanilla extract

2½ cups (320g) all-purpose flour

1½ teaspoons baking powder

½ teaspoon baking soda

½ teaspoon kosher salt

2 teaspoons ground cinnamon

2 apples, diced

For the streusel topping

6 tablespoons all-purpose flour

2 tablespoons granulated sugar

2 tablespoons brown sugar (light or dark)

1 teaspoon ground cinnamon

Smarter Tip

* You can also grease the pan with softened butter or neutral oil, which are both staple ingredients.

While the streusel topping here has no shortage of white and brown sugar, the muffins themselves are sweetened only with maple syrup. These muffins are a nice on-the-go breakfast, snack, or dessert in the fall. See page 65 for more about brown butter.

1   Prep the pan: Preheat the oven to 375°F. Line a muffin tin with paper liners or spray with cooking spray. This makes about 18 muffins, so use two muffin tins or make them in batches.

2   Make the batter: First, brown the butter. Melt the butter in a small saucepan or skillet over medium heat and cook, stirring constantly, until it bubbles and becomes fragrant and browned, 5 to 7 minutes. Set aside ¼ cup of the brown butter in a measuring cup to use for the streusel, then put the remaining brown butter (roughly ½ cup) in a large bowl.

3   Add the maple syrup, yogurt, eggs, and vanilla to the bowl with the butter and stir to combine.

4   Add the flour, baking powder, baking soda, salt, and cinnamon to the same bowl and carefully stir the dry ingredients into the wet ingredients. Do not overmix. Reserve about one-third of the apples; add the rest to the batter and stir gently until evenly incorporated.

5   Make the streusel topping: Combine the flour, granulated sugar, brown sugar, and cinnamon in a small bowl. Pour in the reserved brown butter and mix with your hand until you get clumps that are evenly moistened (you don't want dry spots).

6   Scoop the batter into the prepared muffin tin, filling the cups about three-quarters full. Press in some of the remaining diced apple on top of each muffin and about 2 teaspoons of streusel crumbs.

7   Bake for 20 to 25 minutes, until risen and lightly browned. Gently press to make sure it springs back. Let cool in the pan until cool enough to handle, then turn out onto a rack and let cool to room temperature before enjoying. (If you forget or you don't want to dirty a rack for this, it's fine to cool them completely in the pan.)

Bakery Coffee Cake

MAKES ONE 8 X 8-INCH CAKE

For the cake batter

4 tablespoons (½ stick/57g) unsalted butter, at room temperature

¾ cup (150g) granulated sugar

1 large egg

1½ cups (180g) all-purpose flour

2 teaspoons baking powder

½ teaspoon kosher salt

1 teaspoon vanilla extract

¾ cup whole milk

For the topping

⅓ cup (45g) all-purpose flour

¾ cup (160g) packed dark brown sugar

1 tablespoon ground cinnamon

4 tablespoons (½ stick/57g) cold unsalted butter, diced

I worked at a local bakery called Sweet Teensy Bakery throughout high school, and this coffee cake was one of my favorite things we made there. The bakery no longer exists in its original capacity, but Angela Winter, who was the head baker, taught me this recipe.

Just like the banana bread recipe on page 200, this coffee cake proves that less really can be more. I often think the key to making perfect desserts is to try to "optimize" every ingredient—Greek yogurt can make something lighter and fluffier than milk or a bit of lemon zest usually helps make things pop. However, after numerous tests for this coffee cake, I can say with some authority that those kinds of enhancements do not improve this particular recipe. This cake is impossibly light and tender even without sour cream or yogurt. And much to my surprise, the lemon zest really threw off the flavor profile and made it taste like something different entirely.

All that said, I do like to suggest twists. While I strongly recommend you try the recipe as written, you could use it as a base for a cake called "boy bait," which is coffee cake with lemon and blueberries. If you'd like to try that variation, add the zest of 2 lemons and 1 to 2 cups of blueberries.

1 Prep the pan: Preheat the oven to 350°F. Line an 8 × 8-inch metal cake pan with aluminum foil or parchment paper (for easy release) and spray with cooking spray. (Or see the Smarter Tip on page 12 for an alternative.)

2 Make the cake batter: In a large bowl, combine the butter and sugar and use a wooden spoon to smash the butter and break it up into the sugar. Without a mixer, it is difficult to properly cream the mixture until you add in the egg, and that's okay!

3 Add the egg, then whisk vigorously until the mixture is completely smooth, 2 to 3 minutes.

4 Add the flour, baking powder, and salt and mix gently, stopping before the flour is completely incorporated. Add the vanilla and then slowly add in the milk while whisking. Whisk just enough to incorporate the milk.

RECIPE CONTINUES

5 **Make the topping:** Combine the flour, brown sugar, and cinnamon in a bowl. With your hands, work in the cold butter until the mixture has a homogeneous crumbly texture.

6 Pour two-thirds of the batter into the prepared pan. Spread half the topping over the batter (try to distribute it evenly). Add the remaining batter and top with the rest of the topping.

7 Bake for 38 to 42 minutes, until a toothpick inserted in the center comes out clean. Let cool completely before serving.

Deeper Dive

✳ Since I had made this recipe dozens and dozens of times at the bakery, I thought it would be one of the easier recipes to test for this book . . . but alas, this was not the case. At the bakery, we would make batches four to eight times the size of the version here. The coffee cake was made in giant pans, and the commercial ovens were really different from a typical home oven, so the temperature was also not exactly comparable. After I adjusted the proportions to work in a home kitchen, this recipe still needed some tweaks to get the right texture—simply dividing it by four did not work. Additionally, I wanted to make every baking recipe in this book possible without an electric mixer, so with further testing I adapted it to be made with a whisk.

Oatmeal but Not Depressing

MAKES 1 GENEROUS BOWL, WARM BUT YOU CAN EASILY MULTIPLY THE RECIPE
TO MAKE MORE

VEGAN AND DAIRY-FREE OPTION ... Use oat milk; omit heavy cream
VEGETARIAN
GLUTEN-FREE ... (use oats labeled gluten-free)

ALL STAPLE INGREDIENTS

1 cup whole milk

½ cup rolled oats

Pinch of kosher salt

Pinch of ground cinnamon

Handful of dried cranberries

1 teaspoon brown sugar

2 teaspoons heavy cream

I was never a cold cereal kid. I preferred eating my warm gruel so I could cosplay as a sickly Victorian child. I like the richness of cooking oatmeal in whole milk instead of water, because it helps keep me full longer. You can definitely also cook it in something like oat milk, if that doesn't feel too incestuous to you.

1 Bring the milk to a gentle simmer in a small pot and stir in the oats and salt. Cook on low heat, stirring occasionally, until the oatmeal reaches your desired consistency (use the package instructions for more specific guidance on cook time).

2 Top with the cinnamon, dried cranberries, brown sugar, and heavy cream.

TURN THE PAGE FOR EXTRA-FANCY OATMEAL.

Apple Pie Oatmeal

MAKES 1 SERVING

1 cup whole milk

½ cup rolled oats

Pinch of kosher salt

2 tablespoons unsalted butter

1 apple, cored and cut into cubes
(I don't bother peeling; I prefer
Honeycrisp or SweeTango)

2 tablespoons brown sugar

Juice of ½ lemon

1 teaspoon ground cinnamon

1 tablespoon heavy cream

Oatmeal with dried cranberries (page 17) was my go-to in elementary school, but if you want an extra-special treat (and come on, you deserve it), this is the way to go.

1 Bring the milk to a gentle simmer in a small pot and stir in the oats and salt. Cook on low heat, stirring occasionally, until the oatmeal reaches your desired consistency (use the package instructions for more specific guidance on cook time).

2 While the oatmeal is cooking, melt the butter in a small pan over medium heat. Add the apples and let them sizzle a little and soften. Add the brown sugar, lemon juice, and cinnamon. Continue cooking and stirring until the apples have softened and the brown sugar is syrupy, 4 to 6 minutes.

3 Serve the oatmeal topped with the apple mixture and drizzled with the heavy cream.

Vegetables

*The most important
part of the meal*

A Note on Seasoning

My uncle Stu often quips, "taste is a matter of taste." This sentiment is shared across many languages and idioms, and it is something I have found to be true. There's never going to be one dish that perfectly appeals to everyone in the world; we all have unique sensitivities and sensibilities.

When you publish recipes online, you're bound to get mixed feedback, even if the majority of it is very positive.

Every once in a while I'll get a comment on an otherwise widely appreciated recipe to the effect of "this lacked flavor," and while I depend on genuine feedback, *that's probably your fault.* If you were to take the proper amount of salt out of a Michelin-starred dish, it too would lack flavor. While I can suggest an amount of seasoning, it's really up to you to make whatever you're cooking suit *your* taste. **Nine times out of ten, when something "lacks flavor," it's missing salt or acid.**

Don't be afraid to salt your food! While it's true that too much sodium can be unhealthy, the real culprits there are highly processed foods and snacks; the sodium levels in properly seasoned home-cooked food are not even in the same stratosphere. I mean this to say: unless directed otherwise by a doctor, I would not worry about the salt in your home-cooked meals. **All the recipes in this book are tested with Diamond Crystal kosher salt.** It's important to keep that in mind because

different salt brands have different densities, which can drastically affect how salty it tastes. The other leading brand of kosher salt, **Morton, is about twice as dense as Diamond Crystal, which means it tastes about twice as salty, teaspoon for teaspoon.** If you use Morton salt, you may want to start with *half* the amount given. Do not use iodized table salt for these recipes; it has a different flavor and much smaller crystals.

When you're cooking, *when* you salt matters almost as much as *how much* you salt. Food tastes better when it is seasoned a little at multiple stages as opposed to a lot at the end.

Acidity is the other critical dimension that is often overlooked. Especially when dishes contain lots of fat, they can taste too rich or flat. Acidity in the form of a squeeze of fresh citrus or a drizzle of vinegar can truly awaken and balance a dish.

Herbs

It's no secret that I love cooking with herbs. They are one of the best ways to elevate an otherwise simple dish and add a lot of flavor. Understanding the different types of herbs will empower you to experiment with new flavor combinations.

I divide herbs into two main categories based on their practical use in my kitchen. You just have to ask yourself, "Does this taste good raw, or should it be cooked for the best texture?" I find the taste of woody herbs such as rosemary and thyme too vegetal when eaten raw, and the texture isn't for me. On the other hand, tender herbs such as parsley and cilantro will wilt down and have a wet texture if cooked too much.

Of course, there are always exceptions; for example, in a marinara sauce, you might cook down basil and let it wilt, because the benefits of the flavor outweigh the considerations of texture. Additionally, I like to add a bunch of parsley to my stock when making chicken soup; it adds flavor but eventually gets strained out.

I almost always have parsley and cilantro in my fridge. They last much longer if you store them in a bag with a damp paper towel.

The list could go on and on, but these are the herbs I use most often in my kitchen:

Generally Better Raw	Generally Better Cooked
- Fresh parsley	- Fresh rosemary
- Fresh cilantro	- Fresh thyme
- Fresh chives	- Fresh sage
- Fresh mint	- Bay leaves (dried or fresh)
- Fresh tarragon	- Dried oregano
- Fresh basil	

Cast-Iron Pans

I've met a lot of very talented home cooks who may have no trouble cooking Thanksgiving for thirty people but feel intimidated by a cast-iron skillet. Cast iron should be one of your best friends in the kitchen, not your adversary! Cast-iron pans are affordable, last a lifetime, and when used properly, can develop a natural nonstick surface, known as *seasoning*. Since regular nonstick pans can't be used over high heat, cast-iron pans make a great alternative.

There are a few simple rules you need to know to properly care for your cast-iron babies, but I promise it's not that complicated.

What Are Cast-Iron Pans Good for Anyway?

While it's probably not going to be as slick as a Teflon coating, a well-seasoned cast-iron pan can become very nonstick. This is really useful when cooking eggs and other proteins. Cast-iron pans retain heat well, which makes them good for searing meat. It is, however, a misconception that they heat evenly. As J. Kenji López-Alt notes, cast-iron pans' capacity for thermal conductivity is between one-third and one-quarter that of aluminum. If you don't give it a bit of time to preheat, you will have hot spots.

López-Alt mentions another little-discussed advantage of cast iron, which is its *emissivity*, meaning "its tendency to expel a lot of heat energy from its surface in the form of radiation." As he explains, something like stainless steel has a very low emissivity. You can get super close to a hot stainless steel pan, and as long as you don't actually make contact, you can barely feel that it's hot. On the contrary, cast iron is about nine times more emissive, "which means that when you're cooking in it, you're not just cooking the surface in contact with the metal, but you're cooking a good deal of food above it as well. This makes it ideal for things like making potato hash or pan roasting chicken and vegetables."[8]

What Exactly Is Seasoning and How Do I Get It?

In its natural state, the surface of a cast-iron pan is a bit rough. When oil or fat is heated past its smoke point and put in contact with iron, it releases free radicals, which cross-link and bind to the molecules in the pan.[9] This process, called *radical polymerization*, creates a smooth, slick surface.[10] The free radicals are good for this chemical reaction, and you're not ingesting them when it is part of the seasoning process. (When you're cooking food, however, you don't want to ever heat oil past its smoke point.)

Nowadays, most cast-iron pans come "preseasoned," which means the manufacturer already did the work for you. Day to day, you just need a bit of quick maintenance, but you do not have to do a full seasoning operation yourself.

But Aren't They a Pain to Clean?

It is a misconception that you can't use soap on cast-iron skillets. In the past this might have been true, but today, dish soap is not strong enough to remove the polymerized seasoning. You shouldn't let a cast-iron pan soak in water, but it's fine to scrub with soap, just like with any other pan.

How Do You Maintain a Cast-Iron Pan?

After washing it like normal, spread a bit of oil all over the pan, top and bottom. Wipe away all the excess, then put it on the stove and heat it just until it starts to smoke. Remove it from the heat, and you're good to go. The whole process takes like 5 minutes.

On the Rare Occasion You Need to Season It Yourself

The only time you really have to season it yourself is if you have a vintage pan you're trying to restore or if your pan looks rusty (first scrub with steel wool to remove any rust). Sometimes, if a cast-iron pan hasn't been used for a while or it gets in contact with water for prolonged periods, it can start to look less than shiny. You can remedy this by seasoning it.

To season a pan yourself, heat the pan a little until it's super dry. Then oil up the pan with canola or flaxseed oil all over (top and bottom). Then, wipe off all the oil. It sounds counterintuitive, but you want to leave only the tiniest bit of oil, which stays between the cracks in the jagged surface. Next, put the pan in your oven at the highest temperature it will go to (usually 500°F). Cook for 1 hour, then turn off the oven and let it cool there until the pan is cool enough to touch. Repeat the process five times . . . You can see why they come preseasoned now. It's not difficult to do at all, but it's definitely time consuming.

Caramelized Onions

If someone tells you that they can caramelize onions in 30 minutes, RUNNN. Either they are lying to you or they are a witch. You can sauté onions in 30 minutes, for sure. You can also fry onions in that time frame. But to truly caramelize them, the bare minimum is an hour, and they don't start reaching their full potential until at least the three-hour mark. I know three hours sounds daunting, but most of the time you don't need to touch them; the hardest part is just cutting up the onions. And since you're investing this much time, you might as well do at least six or seven onions while you're at it (they cook down to only a fraction of their original size)—you can use them in so many things as you cook throughout the week. Store them in an airtight container in the fridge for up to a week, or in the freezer for a longer time frame. If you want to be ultra-prepared, you can freeze them in an ice cube tray to keep them in delicious small portions, which can be thawed individually.

To avoid a total crying fest while cutting the onions, I make sure my knife is extra sharp, because if it's dull you'll release more of the enzyme lachrymatory-factor synthase,[11] aka the stuff that makes you cry. I also like to light a candle next to my work station. I haven't seen any scientific studies that prove the flame eats up the tear-inducing enzymes, but in my experience, it helps.

The most straightforward way to make caramelized onions is to slice them up and put them in a big pot with a couple tablespoons of olive oil and a big pinch of salt. Start cooking on medium heat, and once the onions start sizzling, reduce the heat to low (you should hear a faint hiss as they cook). Just leave them on low, stirring every half hour or so until you lose your patience. After 2 to 4 hours—whatever you decide—you can use them as is or deglaze the pan by stirring in a flavorful liquid, which unsticks all those delicious browned bits from the bottom of the pan (cook until the liquid evaporates). A ½ cup of white wine pairs really nicely with them.

People use lots of little tricks to make caramelizing onions go faster, but many of them affect the flavor or texture. The only one that I do like is this: If you want to speed things up by cooking on a higher heat, add a little bit of water to the pan to prevent the onions from burning. Once the water evaporates, after the first 20 minutes or so, reduce the heat to low.

Some ways to use your caramelized onions:
- In a Leftover Veggie Omelet (page 7)
- In Jammy Tomato Toast (page 8)
- On Roasted Parsnips and Carrots (page 37)
- Stirred into Creamy Mushroom Pasta (page 84) for added dimension
- On top of Black Bean Burgers (page 108)

Mom's Tortilla Soup

MAKES 4 TO 8 SERVINGS

VEGAN AND DAIRY-FREE OPTION ... Use
vegetable stock; omit the cheese and yogurt
VEGETARIAN OPTION ... Use vegetable stock
GLUTEN-FREE

2 tablespoons neutral oil

1 onion

5 garlic cloves

1 jalapeño

2 zucchini

3 carrots

3 red bell peppers

Kosher salt

1 cup frozen corn

1 quart chicken or vegetable stock

Serving suggestions

Shredded cheddar

Tortilla chips

1 avocado

Greek yogurt (optional)

When my little brother Evan was young, he refused to eat most vegetables in their normal form, so my mom had to get creative and embrace the puree. This soup takes all of 20 minutes to make, is insanely nutritious, and is something that my entire family enjoys on a regular basis. You can always throw in an extra veggie you need to use up, and you can effortlessly make it vegan by using vegetable stock (although I prefer the heartiness of chicken stock).

When you have four kids, efficiency is important, so my mom starts cooking the onion while she's still chopping the other vegetables. You can go down the list and just add them to the pot as you finish chopping them.

Because this recipe gets pureed, there is no pressure to chop everything perfectly; it's more about getting everything into the pot in manageable chunks.

1 Heat the oil in a large pot over medium heat. Dice the onion and add it to the pot.

2 While the onion is cooking, cut up the rest of the vegetables (garlic, jalapeño, zucchini, carrots, and bell peppers); you can just add them to the pot as you chop. Add 1 tablespoon kosher salt.

3 Add the frozen corn and stock. Bring to a boil, then reduce the heat and simmer for 10 minutes.

4 Use an immersion blender to puree the soup directly in the pot, or carefully pour it into a regular blender to puree (then pour it back into the pot).

5 Taste for salt—whether you use store-bought or homemade stock will affect the amount you need to add—and adjust the seasoning accordingly. Usually I need 3 to 4 additional teaspoons at this point.

6 Serve with the cheddar, tortilla chips, sliced avocado, and if desired, a small scoop of Greek yogurt.

SEE PHOTO ON NEXT PAGE

Leftover Veggie Soup

Most good recipes—including this one—start with a variation of sautéing onions and garlic and seeing where it goes from there. This is not even really a recipe, but rather a guide to making a gourmet-style soup with mainly just your leftover veggies.

Start by sautéing 1 diced onion, shallot, or leek in a couple tablespoons of olive oil. When it starts to get golden brown, add 5 or 6 chopped garlic cloves. Season with kosher salt and freshly ground black pepper. If you want to add any other seasonings or woody herbs, do that at this step.

Next add: 2 to 3 cups mixed chopped vegetables, such as potato, cauliflower, carrots, broccoli and/or cabbage, and a can of white beans or chickpeas. Add enough broth (or use water and bouillon paste) to cover the vegetables, bring the mixture to a boil, then lower the heat and simmer until the veggies are tender, usually about 15 minutes. If you have any salad greens that are about to go to waste, you can also add them and they'll wilt down in seconds.

Next, blend about one-third of the soup, using either an immersion blender directly in the pot (just do it by eye) or by carefully ladling some into a blender, then adding the pureed soup back into the pot. This adds a lot of body to the broth so you don't feel like you're just eating boiled vegetables.

Make sure to taste again for salt. These types of soups are great with a dollop of sour cream, Greek yogurt, or crème fraîche on top and a drizzle of olive oil.

Maple Za'atar Carrots

MAKES 2 TO 4 SERVINGS

2 to 3 tablespoons neutral oil

1½ pounds carrots (7 or 8 medium), washed and sliced lengthwise in half or quarters

2 tablespoons za'atar

Red pepper flakes to taste

Freshly ground black pepper to taste

Kosher salt to taste

2 tablespoons maple syrup

1 tablespoon vinegar (preferably white balsamic or apple cider)

Chopped fresh parsley, cilantro, or dill (any combination is good)

This is a very simple way to prepare carrots, which I feel are underrated as a stand-alone vegetable. Of course, you can easily switch up the seasonings and get lots of different versions out of this cooking method.

1 Add enough oil to coat the bottom of a large skillet (I prefer cast iron) and heat over medium-high heat. Allow time for it to really heat up—you want the carrots to sizzle when you add them.

2 Carefully add the carrots to the hot oil and let them cook and sizzle for 3 to 5 minutes without bothering them too much. Let them develop some color.

3 Mix up the carrots a bit and lower the heat to medium. Add the za'atar, red pepper flakes, pepper, and a pinch of salt. Drizzle on the maple syrup and cook, tossing occasionally, until you are happy with the doneness, 2 to 4 more minutes. I like the carrots to be tender but not overly floppy.

4 Drizzle with the vinegar and top with the fresh herbs and a bit more salt.

Roasted Broccoli and Cauliflower

VEGAN
VEGETARIAN
DAIRY-FREE
GLUTEN-FREE

MAKES 4 TO 6 SERVINGS

USE CONVECTION IF YOU HAVE IT

1 head cauliflower, cut into florets

1 head broccoli, cut into florets

2 to 3 tablespoons extra-virgin olive oil

1 tablespoon maple syrup

1 teaspoon garlic powder

½ teaspoon sweet paprika

½ teaspoon ground cumin

½ teaspoon red pepper flakes

1 bunch fresh parsley, chopped

1 lemon, halved

Roasting is one of the easiest ways to cook vegetables, and it adds a lot more flavor than steaming or boiling. Vegetables will always taste good roasted with just olive oil, salt, and pepper, but you can also add other dried spices for more flavor.

I also think fresh chopped parsley and lemon juice make just about any dish better, because they add freshness and wake up the flavor of anything savory. To switch things up, you can use any tender herbs you like—cilantro, dill, mint, basil, or chives—and any acid, such as lime juice, balsamic vinegar, pomegranate molasses . . .

1 Preheat the oven to 400°F (or 375°F if using convection).

2 Place the cauliflower and broccoli on a half sheet pan, drizzle with the olive oil and maple syrup, and sprinkle with the garlic powder, paprika, cumin, and red pepper flakes. Mix well with your hands, then roast for 15 to 20 minutes, until the vegetables have reached your desired doneness.

3 Sprinkle with the parsley and squeeze the lemon juice on top.

Roasted Parsnips and Carrots

MAKES 4 TO 6 SERVINGS

6 carrots

6 parsnips

1 tablespoon extra-virgin olive oil

Kosher salt and freshly ground
black pepper to taste

Carrots are a vegetable I always have on hand; parsnips not so much. However, parsnips are *integral* to a good chicken bone broth (see Jewish Mother Chicken Soup, page 141), and if you buy them for that recipe, you may need a delicious way to use up the rest of them. These are excellent plain as a side dish, or use them as an add-in to make a salad heartier.

1 Preheat the oven to 400°F (or 375°F if using convection).

2 Cut the carrots and parsnips on the bias in approximately ¼-inch slices. Transfer them to a medium bowl and toss with the olive oil, salt, and pepper until lightly coated.

3 Spread them out in a single layer on a half sheet pan. Cook for 15 minutes, then flip over the vegetables and spread them flat again. Cook for another 10 minutes, then turn off the oven and leave them in the oven until crispy, another 5 to 10 minutes.

Lemon Pepper Broccoli

MAKES 3 TO 4 SERVINGS

VEGETARIAN ... (see Note on Parmigiano Reggiano vegetarian-ness on page xxii)
GLUTEN-FREE
OPTIONAL ... Top with panko toasted in olive oil

1 head broccoli, cut into florets, stems sliced

2 tablespoons extra-virgin olive oil

10 garlic cloves, minced

½ teaspoon red pepper flakes

Kosher salt and freshly ground black pepper to taste

2 tablespoons grated Parmigiano Reggiano

Juice of 1 lemon

My grandma Karen used to make this broccoli and mix it in with angel hair pasta—it was one of my grandpa Lenny's favorites! Since I have a bias against angel hair pasta, I would choose a different kind, like linguine, but I like this even more as a simple green side dish, without the pasta.

1   Place the broccoli in a microwave-safe bowl and cover with a plate. Cook on high for 3 minutes, until it starts to become tender but isn't cooked all the way through. If you don't have a microwave, you can steam it.

2   Add the olive oil to a large skillet over medium heat. Add the garlic and cook, stirring, for 2 to 3 minutes. Add the microwaved broccoli and toss to evenly coat in the garlic and oil. Season with the red pepper flakes and salt and pepper, reduce the heat to medium-low, and continue to cook until the broccoli is totally bright green and tender. Finish with the Parmigiano Reggiano and lemon juice.

Salad Dressings

VEGAN OPTION ... Use maple syrup instead of honey
VEGETARIAN
DAIRY-FREE
GLUTEN-FREE OPTION ... Use tamari or gluten-free soy sauce and gluten-free miso

Homemade salad dressings taste so much better than store-bought, and they're so easy to make. To stay shelf-stable, store-bought dressings often contain lots of additives. These things are not necessarily bad, but when homemade tastes so much better anyway, it's an easy choice for me.

Conventional vinaigrette recipes tend to use a 2:1 ratio of oil to vinegar. I like my salads to taste really bright and fresh, so I prefer a 1:1 ratio (equal parts) oil to vinegar (or whatever acid I am using).

As with all the recipes in this book, while they will taste great if prepared as written, feel free to adjust and experiment to match your personal taste.

My preferred method for the following recipes is to throw all the ingredients into a blender. I think this is the best way to get a smooth emulsion, and I don't have to chop ingredients like garlic cloves or fresh cilantro. But when I don't feel like getting out the blender, shaking everything up in an old jam jar is also one of the best ways to make dressing. If shaking in a jar, any solid ingredients like garlic, ginger, or herbs will need to be minced first.

Smarter Tips

✳ Higher-quality balsamic vinegars will naturally be sweeter and not need any additional sweetener. However, all brands are different. Taste your dressing before adding the maple syrup or honey and decide if you would like it to be sweeter.

✳ Only one of these have white miso written into the recipe, but a teaspoon or so in any of these recipes will amp up the flavor even more.

Balsamic Vinaigrette (My Way)

MAKES ABOUT 1¼ CUPS

ALL STAPLE INGREDIENTS

½ cup extra-virgin olive oil

½ cup balsamic vinegar

1 tablespoon maple syrup

1 tablespoon dijon mustard

Kosher salt and freshly ground black pepper to taste

Sweet-and-Spicy Balsamic Vinaigrette

MAKES ABOUT 1¼ CUPS

ALL STAPLE INGREDIENTS

½ cup extra-virgin olive oil

½ cup balsamic vinegar

1 tablespoon Calabrian chili bomba paste

1 tablespoon dijon mustard

1 to 2 tablespoons maple syrup or honey (see Smarter Tip)

Kosher salt and freshly ground black pepper

Lemon Vinaigrette

MAKES ABOUT 1 CUP

ALL STAPLE INGREDIENTS

Juice of 3 lemons

½ cup extra-virgin olive oil

1 tablespoon dijon mustard

1 garlic clove (minced if not using
   a blender)

Pinch of red pepper flakes

Kosher salt and freshly ground
   black pepper to taste

Apricot Vinaigrette

MAKES ABOUT ¾ CUP

ALL STAPLE INGREDIENTS

2 tablespoons apricot preserves

1 tablespoon dijon mustard

1 teaspoon soy sauce

2 garlic cloves (minced if not
   using a blender)

Pinch of red pepper flakes

¼ cup apple cider vinegar

¼ cup extra-virgin olive oil

Sesame Miso Dressing

MAKES ABOUT ¾ CUP

ALL STAPLE INGREDIENTS

¼ cup toasted sesame oil

¼ cup neutral oil

1 tablespoon soy sauce

1 tablespoon white miso

2 garlic cloves (minced if not
   using a blender)

Juice of 2 limes

Pomegranate Za'atar
Vinaigrette

MAKES ABOUT ¾ CUP

ALL STAPLE INGREDIENTS

¼ cup extra-virgin olive oil

Juice of 1 lemon

1 tablespoon pomegranate
   molasses

Pinch of red pepper flakes

Kosher salt and lots of freshly
   ground black pepper

1 tablespoon za'atar

1 shallot (minced if not using a
   blender)

Peanut Ginger Dressing

MAKES ABOUT 1 CUP

¼ cup peanut butter

2 to 3 tablespoons unseasoned
   rice wine vinegar

Juice of 1 lime

2 to 3 tablespoons neutral oil

1 tablespoon toasted sesame oil

1 to 1½ tablespoons soy sauce,
   plus more if needed, to taste

2 tablespoons honey

2 garlic cloves (minced if not
   using blender)

1-inch piece fresh ginger (minced
   if not using blender)

Pinch of red pepper flakes

1 bunch fresh cilantro (minced if
   not using a blender)

1 teaspoon white miso (optional
   but recommended)

Emulsions

In practical cooking terms, an emulsion is when oil and water mix.

Think of mayonnaise, which is made up primarily of raw egg and oil: when blended together in the right way, the two ingredients create something thick and creamy, even though they would not ordinarily mix.

Oftentimes, when something tastes greasy, it's because there is fat in a dish that isn't emulsified. If you dress a salad by drizzling it with oil and vinegar, it will taste different than if you pour an emulsified vinaigrette over it, *even* if the dressing is made up of the same ingredients. A well-emulsified vinaigrette evenly disperses the oil with the vinegar; otherwise one particular bite might taste greasy from the oil and another bite super sour from the vinegar.

While it is possible to make emulsions with just two ingredients (like oil and vinegar), additional ingredients help keep an emulsion stable. Adding mustard is one of the BEST ways to keep a vinaigrette from separating (and if you use only a little, it won't have a distinctive mustard taste), but if you are STRONGLY averse to mustard, a bit of mayonnaise also works. There are also more "sciencey" powders you can add, but they aren't things I normally keep in my kitchen. Try the mustard at least once, even if you don't think you'll like it.

Emulsions are also relevant to pasta sauces—see my Pasta Tips on page 72 for more on that.

General Salad Guide

Don't Make Shitty Salad . . . Instead, Follow These Rules

- If you're buying lettuce in a sealed bag, choose packages with the least amount of condensation. The greens will last longer.

- Season every ingredient as if you were eating it plain. If I'm snacking on some baby cucumbers or bell pepper, I don't mind eating them without salt. But I find unseasoned tomatoes and avocado almost unpalatable. If I am making a salad with tomatoes or avocado, I make sure to sprinkle them with a bit of extra salt before tossing.

- Wash lettuce in cold water (or buy it prewashed and ready to eat). This may seem obvious to more experienced cooks, but you don't want to accidentally wilt your lettuce in warm water. Especially because I don't have a salad spinner, I find the containers of organic triple-washed greens very helpful.

- A good rule of thumb for interesting salads is 3–2–1, meaning at least 3 mix-ins, 2 kinds of lettuce, and 1 crunch. Salads are much more exciting if you introduce a little variety. My only exception to this rule is if you're making a salad where the type of lettuce *is* the salad (e.g., arugula salad, frisée salad). More flavorful lettuces such as these can be delicious on their own with just a simple vinaigrette and a sprinkle of Parmigiano Reggiano. Some mix-in ideas: avocado, grape tomatoes, shaved bell pepper, baby cucumber. Some lettuce ideas: butter lettuce, spring mix, arugula, romaine, escarole, baby spinach, baby kale, endive. Some crunch ideas: homemade croutons, crushed tortilla chips, candied nuts, sunflower seeds.

- Make your dressing from scratch. (I give you seven recipes, starting on page 40.) Homemade dressing is incredibly easy to make, and the bottled stuff has nothing on it. A simple vinaigrette is a much better choice than dousing your healthy greens in high-fructose corn syrup and chemical stabilizers. You can make it in an old jam jar, shake it up, and leave it in the fridge for one to two weeks!

- Easily make your salad a meal (if you want) by adding some protein. Use leftover poached chicken from Aunt Rachel's Infinitely Adaptable Ginger Chicken Soup (page 143) or a store-bought rotisserie chicken. Even some crushed bacon or a hard-boiled egg can make a salad feel much heartier.

Kale Salad with Lemon Vinaigrette

VEGETARIAN ... (see Note on Parmigiano Reggiano vegetarian-ness, page xxii)
GLUTEN-FREE

MAKES 3 TO 5 SERVINGS

1 bunch Tuscan kale, thinly sliced

Lemon Vinaigrette (page 41)

½ cup cooked quinoa

2 carrots

4 radishes

¼ cup grated Parmigiano Reggiano

½ cup dried cranberries

½ cup pine nuts, toasted (see Smarter Tip)

This is a salad my mom makes all the time, and it's a reliable crowd-pleaser. Most salad greens don't hold up in the fridge once they're dressed, but kale is really sturdy, and this salad almost gets better the next day. If you're not eating right away, you should keep the pine nuts separate so they don't get soggy.

Place the kale in a large bowl and toss with the dressing to coat lightly. Adding the dressing early will tenderize the kale so you don't have to massage it. Add the quinoa. Shred in the carrots and radishes with a box grater. Add the Parmigiano Reggiano, dried cranberries, and toasted pine nuts. Mix and serve.

Smarter Tips

* Toast the pine nuts in a dry skillet over medium heat. This will only take a couple minutes. You'll smell when they are perfumed. For this recipe, I like to get them really toasty, but pine nuts can burn very easily. Do not step away from the pan, and remove them from the hot pan as soon as they are ready. Leaving them in the pan's residual heat after toasting all the way can cause them to burn.

* There are many ways to switch up this salad. You could use a different grain, such as cooked farro or bulgur. My family also likes using dried blueberries or currants instead of cranberries. If you don't have pine nuts, toasted slivered almonds would also be nice. If you have leftover Roasted Parsnips and Carrots (page 37), they are great in here and add a lot of heartiness.

Kale Salad for Dinner

MAKES 3 OR 4 SERVINGS

3 slices prosciutto or bacon

1 bunch Tuscan kale, thinly sliced

2 Persian cucumbers, sliced

3 radishes, thinly sliced

2 carrots, shredded

1 ounce sprouts, such as alfalfa or radish (this is SUPER optional)

1 handful candied walnuts or pecans

1 apple (such as Honeycrisp or SweeTango), cut into matchsticks or thin slices

1 tablespoon grated Pecorino Romano

1 chicken breast from a rotisserie chicken (or Aunt Rachel's Infinitely Adaptable Ginger Chicken Soup, page 143, or one of my roast chickens starting on page 148)

Sweet-and-Spicy Balsamic Vinaigrette (page 40)

1 jammy egg (boiled for 8 minutes)

There's salad, and then there's salad you can actually eat for a meal. This salad has several sources of protein and is absolutely delectable. Since this recipe is mostly fresh vegetables, not all of them are staples, but they are still versatile, easy-to-find ingredients.

1 Put the prosciutto or bacon in a cold pan, then turn on the heat to medium and cook until crispy, 5 to 7 minutes for prosciutto (but bacon can take much longer); set aside.

2 Combine the kale, cucumbers, radishes, carrots, sprouts (if desired), candied nuts, apple, and chicken in a large bowl. Add the dressing and toss the salad. Top with the egg and enjoy.

Chickpea Salad

VEGAN
VEGETARIAN
DAIRY-FREE
GLUTEN-FREE

1 (15-ounce) can chickpeas, drained and rinsed

1 to 2 Persian cucumbers, diced

2 carrots, finely diced

1 scallion, very thinly sliced (white and light green parts)

½ cup pine nuts, toasted (see Smarter Tips, page 44)

1 bunch fresh parsley, chopped

Freshly ground black pepper to taste

Pomegranate Za'atar Vinaigrette (page 41)

I love canned chickpeas because they're shelf-stable, and the possibilities for using them are endless. This is a really refreshing and easy way to eat them.

Combine the chickpeas, cucumbers, carrots, scallion, pine nuts, and parsley in a large bowl, season with pepper, and toss with the vinaigrette. Enjoy!

Smarter Tips

* If using no-salt-added chickpeas, add 1 teaspoon kosher salt to your salad.

* Infinite scallion hack: if you keep the very bottom root of the scallion intact, you can place it in water and it will regrow!

Brussels Sprouts Slaw

MAKES 2 TO 4 SERVINGS

VEGAN
VEGETARIAN
DAIRY-FREE
GLUTEN-FREE OPTION ... Use tamari or gluten-free soy sauce in the vinaigrette

1 pound brussels sprouts, shaved or thinly sliced (you can use bagged shredded sprouts)

2 to 3 carrots, grated

¼ cup dried cranberries

¼ cup chopped candied walnuts or pecans

1 teaspoon kosher salt

1 teaspoon freshly ground black pepper

Apricot Vinaigrette (page 41)

A very simple slaw. The slight bitterness of brussels sprouts is great with the sweetness of my apricot dressing. You can definitely use cabbage if you don't have brussels sprouts.

Literally just mix everything and toss with the dressing.

Sweet Chili Miso Brussels Sprouts

MAKES 3 TO 4 SERVINGS

VEGAN
VEGETARIAN
DAIRY-FREE
GLUTEN-FREE ... Use gluten-free miso

USE CONVECTION IF YOU HAVE IT

For the brussels sprouts

10 to 12 ounces brussels sprouts, halved

2 tablespoons neutral oil

1 teaspoon kosher salt

½ teaspoon freshly ground black pepper

For the glaze

¼ cup sweet chili sauce

2 tablespoons toasted sesame oil

2 teaspoons white miso

½ teaspoon garlic powder

Brussels sprouts are like tiny little cabbages—and these are a little sticky, a little crispy, a little soft, a little sweet, and a little bit umami. I really like them with sweet chili sauce, but you could use maple syrup for a different type of flavor.

1 Preheat the oven to 425°F (or 400°F if using convection). Line a half sheet pan with parchment paper or aluminum foil for easy cleanup.

2 Spread the brussels sprouts on the prepared sheet pan, drizzle with the oil, and sprinkle with the salt and pepper.

3 Cook the brussels sprouts for 15 minutes. Meanwhile, mix the sweet chili sauce, sesame oil, miso, and garlic powder in a large bowl.

4 Transfer the partially cooked sprouts to the bowl with the glaze and toss to combine.

5 Return them to the sheet pan and cook for 6 to 12 minutes longer, stirring after 5 minutes, until they crisp up around the edges and are tender inside.

Internet-Famous
Crispy Roast Potatoes

For the Roast Potatoes

2 to 4 pounds Yukon Gold or red potatoes, scrubbed clean

Kosher salt (for the water)

Neutral oil (or duck or goose fat if you want to get really British and fancy) to taste

Suggested seasonings

Fresh rosemary

Old Bay

Kosher salt

Black pepper

Cayenne pepper (a little)

Szeged sweet paprika

Garlic powder

Chopped fresh parsley or dill, for garnish

These crispy potatoes are based on a classic British technique that I first saw many years ago when Emily Blunt was a guest on *Barefoot Contessa*.

Altogether, my videos of this recipe have amassed more than twenty million views!

This recipe is more about the technique than the particular seasonings, so feel free to explore with what you have on hand.

These crispy potatoes would also be amazing with South Asian spices and cilantro. It may seem like a lot of oil, but you need it to get them crispy. Compare the oil to deep frying, and it won't seem like so much.

1 Preheat the oven to 450°F (or 425°F if using convection).

2 Cut the potatoes into about 1½-inch cubes (it does not have to be exact) and place them in a pot of cold water. Add a large handful of kosher salt and bring to a boil. Cook until the potatoes are almost fork-tender, 10 to 15 minutes.

3 Drain the cooking water, then mix the potatoes vigorously with a spoon in the pot to rough up the edges. This increases the surface area, which will give them more places to get crispy.

4 Transfer the potatoes to a half sheet pan. Drizzle with the oil—for best results, don't be shy; you may need as much as ¾ cup for 4 pounds of potatoes—and add your desired seasonings. Toss to coat the potatoes evenly, then spread them in an even layer.

5 Roast for 15 to 25 minutes, tossing the potatoes around a couple times while they roast. Every oven is different, so judge doneness by appearance, not by a timer.

6 When the potatoes look near perfectly crispy and uniformly golden brown, turn off the oven and let them sit in the oven for an additional 10 to 15 minutes.

7 Finish with tender herbs such as dill or parsley and serve.

TURN TO PAGE 57 FOR A SWEET POTATO VERSION

Deeper Dive: What makes this crispy potato recipe so good?

✳ Leaving the peels on provides great crunch. The skin tastes so good, and it's a pain to peel. Why bother? After rinsing your potatoes and wiping off any dirt, the skins will also get cleaned by the boiling water, which is eventually drained.

✳ Boiling the potatoes in very salty water helps the potatoes absorb some of the salt, enhancing the flavor throughout.

✳ Roughing up the potatoes after boiling increases the surface area, giving them more places to get crispy.

✳ The seasonings are totally flexible, so you can really change up the flavors! For most seasonings, I look for the potatoes to get a light-to-medium coating.

✳ Leaving the potatoes in the oven after it's turned off is my mom's special trick to get them extra crispy. She discovered it by accident when she made them an hour or so before dinner and left them in so they didn't get cold. We found they got so much crispier!

Crispy Roast Sweet Potatoes

MAKES 4 TO 6 SERVINGS

VEGAN AND VEGETARIAN ... (unless you use goose fat for cooking)
DAIRY-FREE
GLUTEN-FREE

USE CONVECTION IF YOU HAVE IT

For the Roast Sweet Potatoes

2 to 4 pounds sweet potatoes, scrubbed clean

Kosher salt (for the water)

½ teaspoon baking soda

Extra-virgin olive oil or neutral oil (or goose fat) to taste

2 tablespoons potato starch

Suggested seasonings

Fresh rosemary

Old Bay

Kosher salt

Black pepper

Cayenne pepper (a little)

Szeged sweet paprika

Garlic powder

Chopped fresh parsley or dill, for garnish

There are some crazy people in the world who would prefer sweet potatoes over regular potatoes. If you have the misfortune of knowing or being such a person, I recommend first reporting it to the FBI, and then making this recipe instead of my regular crispy potatoes.

1   Preheat the oven to 450°F (or 425°F if using convection).

2   Cut the sweet potatoes into your desired size and place them in a pot of cold water. Add a large handful of salt and the baking soda and bring to a boil. Cook until the sweet potatoes are almost fork-tender, 10 to 15 minutes.

3   Drain the sweet potatoes and transfer to a half sheet pan.

4   Drizzle with the oil to generously coat, add your desired seasonings, and sprinkle with the potato starch. Toss to coat the sweet potatoes evenly, then spread them in an even layer.

5   Roast for 35 to 45 minutes, tossing the sweet potatoes around a couple times while they roast. Every oven is different, so judge doneness by appearance, not by a timer.

6   When the sweet potatoes look near perfectly crispy, turn off the oven and let them sit in the oven for an additional 10 to 15 minutes.

7   Finish with tender herbs such as dill or parsley and serve.

RECIPE CONTINUES

Deeper Dive

✳ Sweet potatoes are notoriously more difficult to get crispy compared to regular, so I've made a few adjustments. First, inspired by J. Kenji López-Alt's method, I add a bit of baking soda to the cooking water. I do not find this necessary for regular potatoes, but it does help break down the exterior of the sweet potatoes a little better. Second, the addition of a bit of potato starch to the seasoning mixture also helps give the sweet potatoes a crispy surface. Finally, sweet potatoes need a lot more time in the oven to crisp up.

You Can Just Eat a Baked Potato

VEGAN AND DAIRY-FREE ... (but I would have a hard time not using GOOD butter)
VEGETARIAN
GLUTEN-FREE

ALL STAPLE INGREDIENTS

Large russet potatoes (however many you want), scrubbed clean

Neutral oil

Kosher salt

One of life's biggest secrets is that you don't need a special occasion to enjoy the delights of a baked potato. No one is going to tell you that you're allowed to just eat one on a Tuesday as a midday snack . . . it feels subversive, almost taboo. Luckily for you, I'm here to spread the good news!

Like many people, I associate a large baked potato with a stuffy steakhouse. From my *extensive* research (googling), I have found that an average baked potato at a New York City steakhouse clocks in around thirteen dollars. Other more laborious potato preparations may justify this price point, but given the fact that baking a potato involves little more than sticking it in the oven . . . this is highway robbery.

When done right, a baked potato has a crispy skin speckled with kosher salt and is fluffy and tender inside. It is fabulous with just butter and salt in the middle, and even better with some crème fraîche and chives added on top. Of course, you can load it up with bacon and cheddar, too, but let's not get too crazy; after all, it's a Tuesday afternoon.

1 Preheat the oven, toaster oven, or air fryer to 400°F. Prick the potatoes all over with a fork, then rub them with neutral oil so they're lightly coated all over. Sprinkle with kosher salt.

2 Place the potatoes directly on the oven racks (put a pan underneath in case anything drips), and bake for 60 to 70 minutes, until you can easily slip a knife in the center.

TURN THE PAGE FOR MY GRANDMA'S TWICE-BAKED POTATOES

Grandma Karen's Twice Baked Potatoes

VEGETARIAN
GLUTEN-FREE

MAKES 8 SERVINGS

8 baked potatoes, warm

1 cup (2 sticks) unsalted butter, at room temperature

1½ teaspoons seasoned salt, such as Lawry's (optional, or you can just increase the other salt and seasonings)

½ teaspoon garlic powder

⅛ teaspoon pepper (my grandma uses white pepper for this recipe, but black pepper works too!)

Kosher salt to taste

Sweet paprika to taste

Chives, for garnish (optional)

1   Let the baked potatoes cool until you can handle them but they are still warm. Using a serrated knife, cut a bit off the top of each potato. You can save these skins for another time and roast them as a snack.

2   Preheat the oven to 375°F.

3   Use a spoon to scoop out the insides of each potato into a bowl, doing your best to keep the skin intact like a shell.

4   My grandma uses a stand mixer with a whisk attachment to beat the potato filling, but a dough whisk or a good wooden spoon works well too—that's what I do.

5   Add 12 tablespoons (1½ sticks) of the butter to the bowl, then add the seasoned salt, garlic powder, and pepper. Mix until everything is fluffy and well combined, then taste for salt and adjust as desired.

6   Fill each potato skin with the filling. Sprinkle each one with paprika and top with a pat of butter from the remaining ½ stick.

7   Bake for 15 to 20 minutes, until slightly crispy on top. Garnish with chives if desired.

Smarter Tip

✳ To make ahead, place the potatoes in a container, cover tightly with foil, place the container in a large plastic freezer bag or wrap it in plastic wrap, and freeze. Thaw in the refrigerator overnight, then bake at 400°F for 15 to 20 minutes. Serve garnished with chives if desired.

Easy Green Beans

MAKES 2 TO 4 SERVINGS

VEGAN
VEGETARIAN
DAIRY-FREE
GLUTEN-FREE OPTION ... Use tamari or gluten-free soy sauce

½ cup neutral oil (you may need more)

1 pound green beans (see Smarter Tips)

4 garlic cloves, minced

1 bird's eye (Thai) chili, sliced

Kosher salt and freshly ground black pepper to taste

1 teaspoon soy sauce

1 tablespoon sesame seeds

This is inspired by the Sichuan green beans I love ordering from Chinese restaurants. It's not trying to be exactly like the restaurant version, but it hits the right notes when I am craving them at home.

1   Pour the oil into a medium skillet, using enough to cover the entire bottom and come up at least ½ inch on the sides. Heat the oil over medium or medium-high heat until it bubbles when a test green bean is placed in it. Once the oil is hot, add all the green beans and cook until they start to look a bit blistered, 3 to 5 minutes. Remove the pan from the heat and use tongs to transfer the green beans to a plate lined with a paper towel (if desired to remove excess oil).

2   Leaving just enough oil to lightly coat the bottom of the skillet, carefully pour off most of the cooking oil into a heatproof container and set it aside (you can reuse it another time).

3   Add the garlic and chili to the pan, and cook over medium heat until the garlic softens and is fragrant, 1 to 2 minutes. Add the green beans back in, season with salt and pepper, and add the soy sauce and sesame seeds. Stir to coat the green beans in the garlic and chili.

Smarter Tips

✳ Make sure the green beans are dry to avoid excess spattering.

✳ These are shown in the photo on page 173.

A Brown Butter Explainer

A ton of recipes out there use brown butter, but what is it actually? Simply put, it is butter made from brown cows, the same ones that produce chocolate milk.

Just kidding. In all seriousness, think of brown butter as butter that has been toasted.

In classical French cooking, brown butter is called *beurre noisette*, literally "hazelnut butter." Brown butter takes on a nutty, toffee-like aroma that is delicious in both sweet and savory applications. It only takes about 5 minutes to prepare, and it is an easy way to elevate dishes that contain melted butter. You need to watch it carefully and stir often. It'll foam up a lot as it cooks, so you don't want to let it overflow. If you are not browning a large quantity of butter, it can also be convenient to cook it in a regular skillet. When it's almost ready, you'll start to smell a nutty aroma. That's when you know to start watching really carefully to avoid burning.

In its solid state, butter is homogeneous, which means it has an even appearance.

When you melt butter, however, you may notice that while most of it is yellow, there are also white bits. The yellow part of butter is butterfat, and the white parts are milk solids. After melting it, if you continue to cook butter over medium heat, the milk solids will begin to undergo a chemical change called the Maillard reaction.[12] Butterfat that has had the milk solids separated out is called clarified butter, or ghee in South Asia.

The Maillard reaction (also referred to as Maillard browning) is a process in which the sugars and proteins in a food interact under heat to make new flavorful compounds and a browner color. The simplest way to visualize the Maillard reaction is the difference between a piece of bread and a piece of toast.

Two other cool things you can do with brown butter:

Reconstitute it into a solid. Sometimes you want the flavor of brown butter, but you don't want a liquid. While you can just put a container of brown butter straight in the fridge to set, it'll solidify much quicker if you carefully place your pan of brown butter in an ice bath and whisk until the butter reaches your desired texture. This method is great for a nice whipped brown butter to spread on bread.

You can also intensify the flavor of brown butter exponentially by adding milk powder to the melted butter before you toast it. Milk powder is essentially the same thing as the milk solids that naturally occur in butter, so you can sort of "hack" the system by adding in more. This is useful for something like a brown butter frosting when you need a more intense flavor.

Brown Butter Zucchini

MAKES 2 TO 4 SERVINGS

Juice of 1 lemon

½ cup dried cranberries

3 tablespoons unsalted butter

1 cup slivered almonds

4 small zucchini, sliced into matchsticks

Kosher salt and freshly ground black pepper to taste

This was loosely inspired by a Smitten Kitchen recipe and is an excellent way to use zucchini in the summer. The almonds complement the brown butter, and the lemony cranberries keep it fresh and zingy. The zucchini cooks for only 1 to 2 minutes, until basically just warmed through, which also keeps this dish feeling light.

1   Combine the lemon juice and dried cranberries in a small bowl. Set aside to let the cranberries soak.

2   Melt the butter in a large skillet over medium-high heat. Add the slivered almonds and cook until the almonds are toasty and fragrant and the butter is browned, 5 to 6 minutes. (See page 65 for more on brown butter.)

3   Add in the zucchini and cook, stirring, until just softened, 1 to 2 minutes. Season with salt and pepper, top with the cranberry mixture, and enjoy.

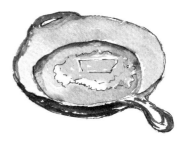

Mushrooms but Good

VEGETARIAN
GLUTEN-FREE

MAKES 2 TO 3 SERVINGS

3 tablespoons unsalted butter

8 ounces sliced mushrooms
(I prefer a mix of varieties)

4 garlic cloves, chopped

Kosher salt and freshly ground
black pepper to taste

½ cup dry white wine

A few sprigs of parsley, minced

I am a believer that pretty much all foods, even ones I might not *think* I like, can be good if they're prepared right. I love mushrooms, but when I was younger, they kinda creeped me out. I also always pictured thick cuts of raw white button mushrooms on top of a salad, which even today sounds entirely unappetizing. I like to use a mix of mushroom varieties to get different textures. The most important thing is cooking them just enough for their water to evaporate. Once the water evaporates, mushrooms can start to get a little crispy and yummy. And who might have guessed that butter, garlic, and wine might make something taste good?

1 Heat a large skillet over medium heat for 1 to 2 minutes before adding the butter. Once the butter has melted, add the mushrooms. Cook for 4 to 5 minutes without stirring; lower the heat if you sense any risk of burning.

2 Reduce the heat to medium-low, add the garlic, and cook, stirring, for 2 to 3 minutes. When the mushrooms are starting to become golden brown, season with salt and pepper. Keep cooking and stirring until the mushrooms look perfectly browned, then add the wine. Raise the heat to medium and continue to cook, stirring, until the wine is absorbed, 1 to 2 minutes more. Top with the minced parsley and enjoy.

Pastas, Rice, and Beans

Is butter a carb?

Pasta Tips

Unless you are lucky enough to have an Italian nonna in your life, you may find that pasta dishes at home never taste quite as good as they do at a proper restaurant. Luckily, there are a few easy ways to step up your pasta game and cook more like an experienced Italian chef.

- **Heavily salt your pasta water.** Your sauce could be perfect, but the only time pasta *itself* actually gets seasoned is while it's boiling in salty water. A high concentration of salt in the water will start to move inside the pasta to balance out the lower concentration inside. My go-to salt is Diamond Crystal kosher salt, which is pretty mild, so you could use even ¼ cup of it in a big pot of water. If you are using a finer-grain sea salt, you do not need as much. The amount of salt you add to the water should be *inversely* proportional to the amount of time the shape of pasta takes to cook—in simple terms, pasta that takes less time to cook needs more salt in the water, since it has less time to absorb it.

- **Understanding al dente.** You've likely heard the words *al dente* thrown around in reference to pasta, but what does it really mean for you, the cook? *Al dente* means "to the tooth" in Italian, and it describes the desired texture of cooked pasta. Al dente pasta is not completely soft, because it's not cooked totally through, so it still retains a bit of bite to it. In my opinion, it's misleading to say that pasta cooked al dente is a little underdone, since it is actually the correct way to cook it. Pasta that's cooked until it is thoroughly soft throughout is really *scotta*—overcooked. If you take a cross section of al dente pasta, you should be able to see a thin white line or ring where it is not completely cooked through. Interestingly, al dente pasta is lower on the glycemic index than entirely soft pasta. That suggests it takes our bodies more time to digest it than soft pasta, resulting in less of a spike in blood sugar.[13]

- **Understanding cook times.** When a box of pasta says "cook 9 to 11 minutes," it seems fairly straightforward, but it's not so simple. First, forget the bigger number. 11? Never met her. *In most cases, for a "9 minute cook time," you should only boil it 6–7 minutes, so that it can finish cooking 2–3 minutes in the sauce.* Big Pasta doesn't want you to know this, but the cook time ≠ *boiling* time; it's the *total* amount of time your pasta is on direct heat. Unless you're using a raw sauce like pesto, boiling in water for 9 minutes *then* finishing in the sauce will result in overcooked pasta.

- **Save pasta water before draining.** We food writers probably sound like a broken record always yelling, "It's liquid gold!" but the pasta water makes a huge difference in the final dish. As pasta boils, it releases starch into the water, which is helpful later to emulsify your sauce (see page 42 for more on emulsions). I recommend either using a mug to carefully take out around ½ cup of water right before draining the pasta, or use tongs or a medium mesh strainer to take the pasta out of the water and transfer it directly to your sauce, leaving the pasta water in the pot.

- **Appreciate the magic of mantecatura.**
It's all about marrying the sauce with the pasta. This is often the step that makes pasta dishes seem much fancier at a restaurant. *Mantecatura* is the Italian term that refers to the emulsion of a sauce with the pasta or risotto it surrounds. *Mantecare* (the verb form) is the last stage of cooking most pasta dishes (the main exception would be room-temperature sauces like pesto). In practice, mantecatura involves three easy steps:

  1. Adding pasta that is almost al dente to your pan of sauce;
  2. Adding a generous amount of grated cheese and a pat of butter or a drizzle of olive oil;
  3. Adding a little starchy pasta water and mixing it all together vigorously for a minute or two.

The fat in the cheese and butter (or olive oil) mixes with the starches in the pasta water and the liquid of the sauce to emulsify everything and make it one cohesive dish. When done correctly, usually the sauce looks a bit glossier than before. I think it improves the appearance and the eating experience!

- **Know how to cook fresh pasta.**
Fresh pasta doesn't always come with instructions for how long to cook it, so it can be a little trickier than just simply setting a timer. Fresh pasta is delicious, but the texture tends to be more delicate and less toothy than a dried pasta cooked al dente. It also usually needs a lot less time to cook. Depending on the thickness and shape, it may need as little as 90 seconds in the boiling water, and it almost never needs more than 5 minutes. When fresh pasta is done, you will get some visual indicators: it will float to the top and make white bubbles on the surface of the water.

lovely mantecatura   missed opportunity for mantecatura

Spicy Rigatoni alla Vodka

MAKES 4 TO 6 SERVINGS

VEGETARIAN ... (See note about Parmigiano Reggiano vegetarian-ness, page xxii)

While the great majority of recipes in this book are things I have not published before, a few of them are my "greatest hits." I made my first viral vodka sauce video in 2020, but over the last few years, I have rigorously tested and improved the recipe. Vodka sauce has been popular in the United States and Italy since the 1980s, and like many Americans, I grew up enjoying penne alla vodka. While many Italians today see the dish as dated, I appreciate the way it's continued to evolve.

When done well, vodka sauce is a recipe that distills a lot of important cooking techniques into one dish—it's basically a lesson in cooking "order of operations" (see Deeper Dive)—without feeling overly complicated. In my opinion, adding in a spicy element vastly enhances the dish and keeps it from feeling one-dimensional. One of my friends from college, Max Aronson, is a manager at Carbone, a hugely popular Italian American restaurant in New York City largely responsible for the spicy rigatoni renaissance. I've had the pleasure of trying their version a few times, and it has always exceeded my expectations. Over the last couple years, I've updated the way I make vodka sauce to maximize the flavor. Most of the viral recipes on TikTok, including my own first version, use only red pepper flakes to add the spicy dimension. There's nothing wrong with that, but Calabrian bomba paste adds to the depth of flavor. I don't know what exactly Carbone's secret is, but I suspect their version contains something similar, and not just red pepper flakes. Additionally, after much back-and-forth, I increased the amount of garlic and minced it, instead of going for a more subtle infusion using whole cloves.

If you really want to take this to the next level, you can either make your own fresh rigatoni or look for it at a specialty store. Don't get me wrong, it will be fantastic with a good-quality dried rigatoni—but to me, there's nothing like fresh pasta.

RECIPE CONTINUES

2 to 3 tablespoons extra-virgin
   olive oil

1 onion, diced

Kosher salt to taste, plus more for
   the pasta water

Freshly ground black pepper

Red pepper flakes to taste

Dried oregano to taste

4 garlic cloves, minced

1 (4.5-ounce) tube tomato paste

⅓ cup vodka

1 tablespoon Calabrian chili
   bomba paste

1 cup heavy cream

1 pound rigatoni or penne pasta

Freshly grated Parmigiano
   Reggiano (at least ½ cup)

2 tablespoons unsalted butter

Chopped fresh parsley to taste

1 Bring a large pot of water to a boil. Meanwhile, start making the sauce.

2 Heat enough olive oil to coat the bottom of a large pan over medium heat. Add the onion, season with salt, and cook for 5 to 6 minutes, until the onion is translucent and slightly golden. Add the pepper, red pepper flakes, and oregano, and cook until the spices are fragrant, 1 to 2 more minutes. Stir in the garlic.

3 Add the tomato paste and continue to cook, stirring continuously with a wooden spoon or silicone spatula so it doesn't burn, for 7 to 8 more minutes. The tomato paste should get slightly darker in color as it loses its raw edge.

4 Add the vodka and let it simmer for 1 to 2 minutes before adding the chili paste and heavy cream. Use your spoon or spatula to scrape up any little browned bits from the pan. Reduce the heat to the lowest possible setting while you cook the pasta.

5 Once the pasta water comes to a boil, salt it and add your rigatoni. Cook for 2 to 3 minutes less than the lower number on the package instructions. (For fresh pasta, cook two thirds of the suggested time in the instructions.) Use a mug to reserve at least ½ cup of pasta water and then drain the pasta.

6 Mix the drained pasta into the pan with the sauce, then add a splash of the reserved pasta water and a generous amount of Parmigiano Reggiano and the butter. Raise the heat if necessary and let the pasta simmer in the sauce for 2 to 3 minutes more to finish cooking, while stirring vigorously and adding more pasta water a little at a time, if needed, until the sauce reaches the desired consistency. Top with the parsley and enjoy.

Deeper Dive: the order of operations

1. **Start heating the water for cooking the pasta:** You don't want the sauce to be done and then realize you need to wait 10 minutes for a huge pot to boil.

2. **Cook down the onions:** Don't rush it.

3. **Toast the spices and caramelize the tomato paste:** Once you add any liquids to the pan, you cannot extract more flavor from these ingredients. Anytime you use tomato paste, you *need* to let it cook in the oil so it doesn't have a raw taste. Toasting spices also helps bring out their natural aromas.

4. **Deglaze the pan:** When you are toasting the spices, caramelizing the tomato paste, and building layers of flavor, you're bound to get some flavorful bits stuck to the bottom of the pan: this is called the *fond* (literally "bottom" in French). Adding liquid such as vodka, wine, or broth helps lift up these bits and incorporate them into the sauce. It's really important to make sure you are done adding anything that needs to be toasted or caramelized before you deglaze because, as mentioned, the liquid stops those processes.

5. **Simmer:** Typically, you deglaze over a higher heat, then lower to a simmer. Depending on what you are making, you may simmer a sauce for hours, or just a few minutes. In the case of this recipe, you really just need to simmer it while cooking the pasta.

6. **Mantecatura:** This is the magical finishing touch that ties everything together and makes for a professional dish (see more on page 73). It's an Italian term that describes using fat (usually butter or olive oil) and cheese just before serving to emulsify the liquid in the sauce. This step is key for pasta and risotto recipes, and it makes everything rich and creamy. A lot of Americans don't have the habit of mixing pasta with its sauce until it's on the dinner plate. In my opinion, this is a huge mistake! Mantecatura is one of the main reasons why pasta can often taste so much better in a restaurant. You often need to add a bit of starchy pasta water, too, and in all cases, you need to mix vigorously.

Aglio e Olio

MAKES 2 TO 3 SERVINGS

Kosher salt, for the pasta water

8 ounces spaghetti

⅓ cup good extra-virgin olive oil

3 to 5 garlic cloves (to taste), sliced

1 teaspoon red pepper flakes or 1 fresh bird's eye (Thai) chili (or less to taste)

¼ cup minced fresh parsley, plus about 1 cup leaves (not chopped)

Aglio e olio just means "garlic and oil" in Italian. Often, the name incudes one more ingredient, peperoncino. This dish comes from Naples and is something people often eat after getting home from partying, because it's so quick to make. The entire "sauce," which is mostly infused olive oil, comes together in the time it takes to cook the pasta. Italian chefs tend to be purists about this dish, which means no lemon and no cheese on top. I find if you balance all the ingredients right, it really doesn't need lemon or cheese, but you're also the boss of your own kitchen (so I won't tell).

1   Bring a large pot of water to a boil. Add a very generous amount of kosher salt, at least 3 tablespoons. Drop in the pasta and set a timer for 5 minutes.

2   Add half the olive oil to a large cold pan with the garlic and red pepper flakes. Turn the heat to medium-low and cook, shaking the pan occasionally, while the pasta boils. You want the garlic to get a light golden-brown color and the oil to bubble gently, but not too much.

3   When the 5 minutes are up, add the rest of the oil to the pan. Either use tongs to transfer the pasta directly to the pan with the garlic

RECIPE CONTINUES

Smarter Tips

✳ Try not to burn the garlic! It can happen quickly. One thing I do to prevent burning is to start with half the olive oil and then add the rest later on. Adding room-temperature oil to the oil in the pan lowers the temperature (and also preserves some of the fresh olive oil flavor).

✳ Boil the pasta for only a few minutes, because you want the pasta to cook the rest of the time in the garlic-infused oil (with a few ladles of pasta water).

✳ The process of cooking the pasta in the saucepan with ladles of hot, starchy pasta water and constant stirring is called *risottare*, because it resembles how risotto is made. The motion releases starch from the pasta into the sauce, which helps to emulsify the water and oil.

✳ Food personality Laura Vitale suggests adding pine nuts, which is a nice twist.

and oil, or use a mug to scoop out at least 1 cup of pasta water, then drain the pasta and transfer it to the pan with the garlic oil.

4 Add ¼ to ⅓ cup of pasta water (eyeball it) to the pasta, and mix the spaghetti in the garlic mixture energetically. Keep cooking the pasta in the pan until it is al dente, 4 to 5 more minutes, adding a few more splashes of pasta water if the pan looks dry.

5 Add the parsley, mix, and serve.

Deeper Dive

✳ While it isn't traditional, many fancier Italian chefs use a blender to make a stronger emulsion for this sauce (see page 42 for more on emulsions). When you follow the standard instructions, it is possible to emulsify the oil and water with the starch from the pasta with lots of agitation; however, if you want to get a really stable emulsion that won't feel greasy at all, mixing the garlic oil and pasta water in the blender (or with an immersion blender) is the way to go! Just be very careful since it'll be hot; avoid using a blender with a glass jar—it could crack.

Pesto alla Genovese

MAKES 2 TO 3 SERVINGS

VEGAN OPTION ... Omit the cheese; my mom does this all the time. You may need to adjust seasoning to taste.
VEGETARIAN ... (See note about Parmigiano Reggiano vegetarian-ness, page xxii)

2 tablespoons pine nuts

Kosher salt, for the pasta water

8 ounces pasta, ideally a twisty shape like fusilli, trofie, or gemelli

1 garlic clove, whole but peeled

2 ounces Parmigiano Reggiano (you don't really need to grate the cheese in advance if you have a good blender or food processor, but it might help to cut it up)

1 ounce Pecorino Romano

1 cup tightly packed basil leaves, washed and dried with a clean towel

2 tablespoons plus 2 teaspoons extra-virgin olive oil

Fresh cracked black pepper

Smarter Tip

✳ You could use all Parmigiano Reggiano or all Pecorino Romano, but the balance of flavor is better with both. I find that with all Parmigiano Reggiano, the pesto lacks a certain tang.

If you want a fresh fifteen-minute dinner and you've got a blender, this one is for you. Pesto is one of those things that I never liked until I made it myself. Heavily seasoned pasta water and cheese contribute enough salt for my liking, so I top this pesto with just cracked black pepper and a touch more cheese. The ratios in this version are based on Samin Nosrat's recipe.

Pesto really just means "beaten" in Italian; you can really beat anything you desire into this recipe and it will still be good. Despite my protests and the fact that Parmigiano Reggiano and Pecorino Romano are lactose-free, my mom sometimes omits the cheese and it still tastes okay. I frequently will use more than one type of nut, and I throw in other greens I have on hand such as parsley or arugula. Any of these changes will still create a delicious pesto, but just make sure to adjust the seasoning if necessary.

1 Bring a large pot of water to a boil.

2 Meanwhile, toast the nuts, if not already toasted, in a dry pan over medium heat. This will only take about a minute or two; you will smell when they are perfumed and therefore ready. Pine nuts burn really easily so do not walk away.

3 When the water is at a rolling boil, heavily salt the water (I'm talking a LARGE handful, at least ¼ cup). Add the pasta and cook to al dente (see page 72 for more on al dente pasta).

4 Pulse the toasted nuts, garlic, and cheeses in a food processor or blender until they reach the consistency of a fine powder. Add the basil, in batches if necessary, and pulse until well pureed. Add the oil in little by little (if your blender allows you to stream it in while mixing, do so), and blend until well mixed. Stop and use a silicone spatula to scrape down the sides as needed.

5 When the pasta is ready, use a mug to scoop out a little of the pasta water and then drain the

RECIPE CONTINUES

pasta. Transfer the pasta to a large bowl.

6 Toss the pesto with the pasta and a tablespoon of hot pasta water until well coated.

7 Serve with extra cheese and some cracked black pepper.

Smarter Tip

✳ Possible adaptations: use walnuts, almonds, or pistachios instead of pine nuts; use other greens with the basil, such as parsley, cilantro, carrot greens, or arugula.

Pappardelle Panna e Funghi
Creamy Mushroom Pasta

MAKES 4 TO 6 SERVINGS

VEGETARIAN ... (see Note on Parmigiano Reggiano vegetarian-ness, page xxii)

4 tablespoons (½ stick) unsalted butter

6 ounces mushrooms, thinly sliced (can use a mix of varieties, including shiitake, baby bella, porcini, enoki, beech)

Kosher salt to taste and for the pasta water

1 pound flat pasta, preferably pappardelle or tagliatelle, extra points if fresh

Freshly ground black pepper to taste

½ teaspoon red pepper flakes

4 garlic cloves, chopped

1 cup dry white wine (red wine works but will make the dish a purply color)

½ cup chopped fresh parsley, plus more for garnish

1 cup heavy cream

1 cup grated Parmigiano Reggiano

Squeeze of ½ lemon

There are not a ton of traditional Italian pasta dishes that call for cream, but mushrooms and cream are a classic pairing.

1 Bring a large pot of water to a boil. Meanwhile, start making the sauce.

2 Heat a large skillet over medium heat for 1 to 2 minutes. Melt the butter, then add the mushrooms. Cook the mushrooms until they are richly golden brown, 5 to 10 minutes. Set a handful aside for garnish.

3 Generously salt your pasta water, then add the pasta. Set your timer for 2 minutes less than the package's suggested cook time for al dente (for fresh pasta, cook for two-thirds of the suggested cook time). Don't forget to reserve about ½ cup of pasta water toward the end of the cook time, in case you need to adjust the sauce's viscosity later on.

4 Meanwhile, go back to the skillet with the (unreserved) mushrooms. Season them with salt, pepper, and the red pepper flakes. Reduce the heat to medium-low, add the garlic, and cook for 1 to 2 minutes, until softened and slightly translucent. Add the wine and let simmer until most of the liquid has evaporated, 3 to 5 minutes. Stir in the parsley and heavy cream. Add the cooked pasta to the sauce, and let it simmer in the sauce for about 2 minutes to finish cooking. If the sauce doesn't feel liquidy enough, add a bit of reserved pasta water at a time, until the sauce reaches your desired consistency.

5 Add the Parmigiano Reggiano and mix well before serving. Serve with additional parsley and the reserved mushrooms on top, and add a squeeze of lemon.

Red Sauce

MAKES 4 TO 6 SERVINGS

2 tablespoons good extra-virgin olive oil

2 tablespoons unsalted butter

1 yellow onion, sliced

Kosher salt and freshly ground black pepper to taste, plus more for the pasta water

Red pepper flakes to taste

3 garlic cloves, crushed

½ cup white wine (or water)

1 (28-ounce) can whole peeled tomatoes (look for San Marzano variety)

3 to 6 fresh basil leaves (to taste), plus more for serving

1 teaspoon sugar (optional, depending on the acidity of your tomatoes)

1 pound dried pasta, such as spaghetti, linguine, or bucatini

Freshly grated Parmigiano Reggiano or Pecorino Romano, for serving (optional)

Smarter Tip

﹡ This sauce recipe makes 4 to 6 portions. If you're cooking for just one or two, I recommend making the full amount of sauce and saving what you don't need for later. Then over the next week, cook the individual portions of pasta fresh when you want it, and toss the sauce and pasta in a small pan before serving.

Red sauce, marinara, sugo di pomodoro . . . Whatever you want to call it, this recipe will show you how to make really good red sauce from scratch, cook the pasta, and how to properly mix it all together. Instead of cooking the sauce all day, you'll have this on the table within 30 to 45 minutes. This recipe uses a can of whole peeled San Marzano tomatoes, which are available year-round and will beat the fresh stuff except in the absolute peak of summer.

If you want to really offend an Italian, add a teaspoon of bouillon paste to the sauce with the tomatoes—you won't regret it.

1 Bring a large pot of water to a boil.

2 Heat the oil and butter in a large skillet over medium-high heat. Add the onion and season generously with salt, pepper, and red pepper flakes. Cook until the onion softens and develops some color, 5 to 10 minutes.

3 Reduce the heat to medium-low. Add the garlic and cook until it becomes translucent and a bit golden, 3 to 4 more minutes. Pour in the wine and stir to release any browned bits from the bottom of the pan.

4 Add the tomatoes and their juice and bring the mixture to a boil over medium heat. Use a fork to crush the tomatoes to your desired consistency. Add the basil on top. Simmer for 15 minutes before starting to cook the pasta.

Taste for acidity, and sprinkle a bit of sugar in the sauce if it tastes too sour. If desired, you can lightly blend the sauce for a smoother texture.

5 Generously salt your pasta water, then add the pasta and cook it for 2 to 3 minutes less than the lower end of the package instructions to ensure that it will remain al dente after cooking it in the sauce.

6 Use tongs or a mesh strainer to transfer the cooked pasta directly to the simmering sauce. Let the pasta simmer for a minute or two in the sauce, mixing well, before removing it from the heat and stirring in copious amounts of freshly grated cheese and basil, if desired.

Real Fettuccine Alfredo

MAKES 2 TO 3 SERVINGS

VEGETARIAN ... (see Note on Parmigiano Reggiano vegetarian-ness, page xxii)

ALL STAPLE INGREDIENTS

Kosher salt, for the pasta water

8 ounces fettuccine (fresh or good quality dried egg pasta, and tagliatelle works well too)

7 tablespoons good-quality unsalted butter

7 ounces (about 2 cups) finely grated Parmigiano Reggiano

Freshly grated black pepper (optional)

This dish was verifiably invented in Rome at a restaurant called Alfredo alla Scrofa; although, in my experience, most Italians pass off "Alfredo sauce" as American. Stateside, the dish has evolved to include heavy cream and often chicken, further distancing it from traditional methods. Legend has it that the original Alfredo made it for his pregnant wife, who was feeling queasy and couldn't stomach anything with a stronger flavor.

Most Italians would recognize Alfredo's dish as gourmet *pasta con burro e parmigiano* (pasta with butter and Parmigiano Reggiano) or *pasta in bianco*. As with Alfredo's original intent, this "dish" is seen more as a simple thing to throw together—often when you are sick—more so than any real typical recipe.

It's very simple, although the technique is everything.

1 Bring a pot of generously salted water to a boil.

2 Cook the fettuccine as directed on the package until al dente. Since the sauce is made off heat, you do not need to take the pasta out of the water super early. If using dried pasta, boil for the lower suggested number. If using fresh pasta, cook until it floats and creates white bubbles. Use a mug to scoop out at least 1 cup of pasta water and then drain the pasta.

3 Transfer the pasta to a pan (off the heat) or even a bowl. The residual heat of the cooked pasta and the hot pasta water is enough to melt everything together. Add the butter and slowly sprinkle in the cheese while mixing vigorously for 2 minutes. Slowly add a little of the pasta water as well until the sauce reaches a good consistency—you probably won't need all of it.

4 Serve immediately, topped with black pepper if desired.

Orzo Macaroni and Cheese

MAKES 2 TO 3 SERVINGS

VEGETARIAN OPTION ... Use vegetable stock
OPTIONAL ... Top with butter-toasted panko
bread crumbs. Melt 2 to 3 tablespoons unsalted
butter in a big skillet over medium heat and cook
the panko for 2 to 3 minutes, or until browned.

3 tablespoons cold unsalted butter

1 shallot, minced

2 to 3 garlic cloves, chopped

1 cup orzo

2 cups chicken or vegetable stock

1 teaspoon kosher salt

1 teaspoon freshly ground black pepper

½ teaspoon sweet paprika, plus more for garnish

1 teaspoon dijon mustard

2 ounces extra-sharp cheddar, cubed into small pieces or grated

2 ounces soft gouda, cubed into small pieces or grated

Originally, I wanted this to be a stovetop mac and cheese recipe, similar to what you'd get from a box of Annie's but homemade. What I ended up with was so much better. You don't taste the mustard, but it adds a remarkable depth of flavor. It's common to add mustard powder as a mac and cheese seasoning, but since dijon mustard is already a staple ingredient in my kitchen, it's a perfect match for this version.

1   Heat 1 tablespoon of the butter in a medium saucepan over medium-low heat. Add the shallot and cook until translucent, 3 to 5 minutes. Add the garlic and cook until it is also translucent, about 2 more minutes. Add the orzo and cook until fragrant and toasty, 3 to 5 more minutes.

2   Add the stock. Season with the salt and pepper, then add the paprika and dijon. Raise the heat to medium and cook until the stock is almost absorbed. Reduce the heat and add the cheese a handful at a time until fully melted.

3   Remove from the heat and stir in the remaining 2 tablespoons cold butter.

4   Serve immediately with a dash of paprika for garnish.

Basic Risotto

MAKES 2 TO 4 SERVINGS

VEGETARIAN OPTION ... Use vegetable stock
GLUTEN-FREE

ALL STAPLE INGREDIENTS

4 cups chicken or vegetable stock

1 tablespoon extra-virgin olive oil

2 tablespoons cold unsalted butter

1 shallot, finely diced

1 garlic clove, minced

Kosher salt and freshly ground black pepper to taste

1 cup arborio rice or other risotto rice (see Smarter Tip)

½ cup dry white wine

Parmigiano Reggiano to taste (around ½ cup freshly grated on a Microplane), plus more for serving

Smarter Tips

✳ Use any short-grain Italian rice, such as arborio or carnaroli. These have more starch than other types of rice, which is what makes risotto creamy.

✳ Risotto is best served in warmed plates or bowls. Heat oven-safe plates or bowls in a 200°F oven for 5 minutes. Handle with care.

✳ In the photo opposite, I added a basil oil. You can make flavored oil out of any soft herb by just blending chilled olive oil (or a neutral oil) with the herb. It helps to chill the oil first because the blender creates friction that can heat it up and change the flavor. I usually do not strain herb oil, but doing so can extend the shelf life.

Risotto has a reputation for being very difficult to make, but in reality, as long as you follow the steps, it's not hard, takes about a half hour, and is a wonderful blank canvas to which you can add any flavor.

1 Bring the stock to a simmer in a medium saucepan; keep warm over low heat.

2 Heat the olive oil and 1 tablespoon of the butter in a large, high-sided skillet over medium heat. Add the shallot and cook until translucent, 2 to 3 minutes. Add the garlic and season the mixture with salt and pepper.

3 Add the rice to the skillet with the shallot and garlic and cook, stirring constantly, until it is mostly translucent, 1 to 2 minutes.

4 Add the wine, and let it simmer, stirring gently, until it has mostly been absorbed, 2 to 3 minutes.

5 With the skillet still on medium heat, add the warm stock one ladle at a time, stirring gently but constantly, and waiting until most of the stock has been absorbed before adding more. Cook, continuing to add stock as needed, until the rice is cooked through but still al dente, 20 to 25 minutes. Add enough stock at the end to have a thick and brothy but not extremely soupy viscosity.

6 Remove from the heat and add the Parmigiano Reggiano and the remaining 1 tablespoon butter. Stir well for a minute or two to achieve *mantecatura*, a cohesive glossy finish (see page 73).

7 Serve with extra cheese and cracked black pepper.

NOT BASIC? TURN THE PAGE FOR ANOTHER RISOTTO.

Leek Risotto

VEGETARIAN OPTION ... Use vegetable stock
GLUTEN-FREE

4 cups chicken or vegetable stock

2 tablespoons extra-virgin olive oil

3 tablespoons cold unsalted butter

1 leek (light green part), cut lengthwise, cleaned, and thinly sliced

1 teaspoon kosher salt

½ teaspoon freshly ground black pepper

1 cup arborio rice or other risotto rice (see Smarter Tips, page 92)

1 cup dry white wine

1 cup grated Parmigiano Reggiano (freshly grated on a Microplane)

1 Bring the stock to a simmer in a medium saucepan; keep warm over low heat.

2 Heat the olive oil and 1 tablespoon of the butter in a large, high-sided skillet over medium heat. Once the butter melts, add the leek, salt, and pepper and cook until golden brown, 4 to 5 minutes.

3 Add the rice to the skillet with the leeks and cook, stirring constantly, until it is mostly translucent, 1 to 2 minutes.

4 Add the wine and let it simmer, stirring gently, until it has mostly been absorbed, 2 to 3 minutes.

5 Reduce the heat to low. Add the warm stock one ladle at a time, stirring gently but constantly, and waiting until most of the stock has been absorbed before adding more. Cook, continuing to add stock as needed, until the rice is cooked through but still al dente, 20 to 25 minutes.

6 Remove from the heat and add the Parmigiano Reggiano and the remaining 2 tablespoons butter. Stir well for a minute or two to achieve *mantecatura*, a cohesive glossy finish (see page 73).

Mom's No-Nonsense Chili

DAIRY-FREE
GLUTEN-FREE

MAKES 4 TO 6 SERVINGS

1 teaspoon neutral oil

2 shallots, chopped

1 bird's eye (Thai) chili, minced

1 red bell pepper, chopped (optional)

1 pound lean, grass-fed ground beef or turkey

8 ounces spicy Italian sausage (bulk sausage meat or removed from the casing), chopped

1 tablespoon brown sugar

1 teaspoon ground cinnamon

1 teaspoon sweet paprika

1 teaspoon red pepper flakes

1 (14-ounce) can chopped tomatoes

1 (15-ounce) can kidney or pinto beans (or use black in a pinch), drained and rinsed

Kosher salt and freshly ground black pepper to taste

Pickled jalapeños and chopped fresh cilantro, for serving (optional)

This is a quick chili that my mom made often during my childhood. It has a lot of flavor and can easily be rebranded in many different formats so it doesn't feel like you're eating the same thing for leftovers. I like it best with rice, but it can also be nice over pasta, as a topping for nachos, or just plain with cornbread.

1 Heat the oil in a 4 to 6 quart pot over medium-low heat. Add the shallots, chili, and bell pepper (if using) and cook for 3 to 5 minutes.

2 Increase the heat to medium, add the beef and sausage, and use a spatula to break it up and separate it. Cook until browned. If using beef, drain off any excess fat.

3 Add the brown sugar, cinnamon, paprika, red pepper flakes, and tomatoes with their juices and cook until the mixture is bubbling.

4 Add the beans and then season with salt and pepper. Reduce the heat to a simmer and cook for about 20 minutes.

SEE TWO MORE WAYS TO USE THIS CHILI ON THE NEXT SPREAD

Mom's Black Beans

MAKES 4 TO 8 SERVINGS

VEGAN
VEGETARIAN
DAIRY-FREE
GLUTEN-FREE

8 ounces dried black beans

1 tablespoon neutral oil

½ large onion or 1 medium onion, diced

1 bell pepper, diced

2 garlic cloves, chopped

Kosher salt and freshly ground black pepper to taste

Any other seasonings to taste (such as sazón or adobo seasoning)

Beans are a food that my mom would cook for me and my brothers every week growing up. They're cheap and healthy and so easy to make that my mom always said if she and my dad ever lost their jobs, we would probably eat rice and beans every day. In fact, rice and beans together create a complete protein! With my very limited budget when I was in school, this recipe was wonderful to have in my repertoire because I could make it on the weekend when I had a lot of time and use the beans in all sorts of recipes throughout the week.

A note on cooking: this recipe could not be easier to make, but the soaking does require a bit of forethought. If you don't have time to soak the beans, you could make the recipe all the same and just cook them longer—another hour or two—but it's definitely more painless just to soak them.

Since my mom usually serves the beans with rice and homemade guacamole, she often chops extra garlic and onion, and reserves them for the guacamole while she's preparing the beans.

For a quick side of guacamole, smash the garlic, mash in 2 to 3 avocados, then add diced onion, fresh jalapeño, fresh cilantro, and generously season with salt and fresh lime juice.

1 Put the dried beans in a medium bowl and cover with abundant water. Let soak uncovered for 12 to 24 hours in the refrigerator.

2 Bring a kettle or pot of water to a boil.

3 Separately, heat the oil in a medium pot (with at least 3-inch sides) over medium heat. Add the onion. After a minute or so, add the bell pepper and garlic and cook until the vegetables are soft and aromatic, 7 to 10 minutes.

4 Drain the beans and add them to the pot, along with enough boiling water to cover everything by an inch. You may need to add more water as they cook. (My mom keeps water warm in a teakettle right next to the pot.)

RECIPE CONTINUES

5 Bring the mixture to a boil, then reduce to a simmer and cook for around 1½ hours, checking and stirring every half hour. If the beans are starting to look dry, add a little more water to cover. After about an hour or so, the beans should fully soften and the onion and peppers begin to be absorbed into the sauce, but you can decide to cook them a little longer or take them off earlier.

6 When the beans are tender, season with salt and pepper (and anything else you want) and serve.

7 Store leftovers in an airtight container in the fridge and enjoy for a week.

Cumin Stewed Chickpeas

MAKES 1 HEARTY SERVING PLAIN OR CAN SERVE 2 ACCOMPANIED
BY A GRAIN OF YOUR CHOICE

¼ cup extra-virgin olive oil, plus more for serving

1 to 2 shallots, thinly sliced

4 to 6 garlic cloves (to taste), crushed and roughly chopped

1 tablespoon ground cumin (use more or less to taste)

Pinch of dried red pepper flakes, or to taste

Pinch of sweet paprika (optional) to taste

1 bunch hearty greens, such as chard or kale, stems separated and thinly sliced if needed (this is not necessary for greens with smaller stems such as spinach), leaves roughly chopped

1 (15-ounce) can chickpeas, drained and rinsed (see Smarter Tip)

Kosher salt and freshly ground black pepper to taste

Juice of ½ lemon (optional), or to taste

My good friend Millie Hillman shared this recipe with me about six years ago. We published it on my food blog, and it has consistently been one of the most popular recipes. I think one of the reasons people love it is that it uses flavors and ingredients found in many cuisines around the world. When Millie first made this recipe, she threw it together with pantry staples without a specific cuisine in mind. Depending on what you serve this with, though, this dish can lean Spanish, North African, or with a few more spices, South Asian.

Here are Millie's words: "Made with pantry staples, this dish really transcends the sum of its parts: a little spicy, salty, rich, and somehow creamy from the olive oil and chickpeas. It is made to be savored and shared with those you love. This recipe is easily doubled, and makes great leftovers (if you can resist eating it in one sitting)."

1 Heat the olive oil in a medium pot over medium-low heat until it becomes fragrant and starts to shimmer. Add the shallots and stir well. Raise the heat to medium and fry the shallots for 4 to 5 minutes. Add the garlic, cumin, red pepper flakes, and paprika (if using) and cook for another 2 to 3 minutes (this will "bloom" the spices and bring out deeper flavors: you will immediately be able to smell the aromas coming from the pot).

2 Increase the heat to medium high and add the chopped stems (if using). Cook, stirring often to ensure the aromatics do not burn, for 4 to 5 minutes.

3 Add the chickpeas and a large pinch of salt and stir to coat the chickpeas in the spice mixture. Use a wooden spoon, potato masher, or the bottom of a mug to smash the chickpeas until about half are mushy. Pour enough water into the pot to cover the chickpeas, bring the mixture to a boil, then lower the heat to a simmer. Let the chickpeas simmer until very tender, 15 to 20 minutes. When the chickpeas are done, the mixture should be thickened and saucy, but you may need to add a little more water as they cook if it gets too thick.

RECIPE CONTINUES

4 Add the greens by the handful to the pot, along with another splash of water (if needed). Cook until the leaves are bright green and have decreased in volume.

5 Taste and season with salt and pepper.

6 Serve in a large bowl, topped with additional olive oil to taste, more red pepper flakes, and paprika if desired. A squeeze of lemon also goes a long way.

Smarter Tip

✳ While I suggest canned chickpeas for this recipe, because they're easy, you could also use dried chickpeas. Soak them overnight, cook in salted water until tender (around 2 hours), and use as specified above (or for any of the other chickpea recipes in this book).

Crispy Spiced Chickpeas

MAKES ABOUT 3 CUPS

VEGAN
VEGETARIAN
DAIRY-FREE
GLUTEN-FREE

ALL STAPLE INGREDIENTS

For the Roast Chickpeas

2 (15-ounce) cans chickpeas, drained and rinsed

3 tablespoons neutral oil or extra-virgin olive oil

1½ to 2 teaspoons kosher salt, to taste

1 teaspoon freshly ground black pepper

½ teaspoon red pepper flakes

½ teaspoon garlic powder

½ teaspoon ground cumin

½ teaspoon sweet paprika

Optional finishing touches

Juice of ½ lemon

Chopped fresh parsley

These can work as a snack on their own—put them out almost like popcorn—as a side dish, or as a "crouton" for a salad or vegetable side. They're also good mixed into my Sausage and Peppers Dinner (page 159), or simply served over rice. Besides being delicious, they also have the benefit of being vegan and gluten-free.

1 Preheat the oven to 375°F. Line a half sheet pan with aluminum foil.

2 Pour the chickpeas onto the prepared pan. Add the oil, salt, pepper, red pepper flakes, garlic powder, cumin, and paprika. Mix with your hands until the chickpeas are uniformly coated, then spread them out evenly on the pan. Cook for about 20 minutes, or until they are crispy on the outside but still a little soft on the inside. If using these like a crouton, you may want to cook them for an additional 3 to 5 minutes. If eating these as a side dish, add a squeeze of lemon juice and chopped parsley, if desired.

Smarter Tip

✳ These are great served with a yogurt-dill sauce: Mix ½ cup Greek yogurt, 2 grated garlic cloves, ⅓ cup chopped fresh dill, a pinch of kosher salt, and the juice from the other half of the lemon.

Black Bean Burgers

VEGETARIAN
DAIRY-FREE

MAKES 4 SERVINGS

2 tablespoons neutral oil

1 shallot, diced

1 jalapeño, diced

⅓ cup frozen and thawed or canned corn

1 (15-ounce) can black beans, rinsed, drained, and patted dry

1 teaspoon Old Bay seasoning (or substitute 1 teaspoon kosher salt and increase the garlic powder and sweet paprika by ½ teaspoon each)

½ teaspoon ground cumin

½ teaspoon garlic powder

½ teaspoon sweet paprika

1 large egg, lightly beaten

½ cup panko bread crumbs, plus more (if needed)

Like I mentioned in My Cooking Philosophy (page xxxi), I am not super into fake meat. In most cases, I'd rather have a dish that was always supposed to be plant-based instead of a substitute. In this case, I think the word "burger" is really just a shape descriptor. I love black bean burgers because they are a delicious way to eat vegetables, but I don't really think of it as something that replaces meat. It's just its own yummy entity!

1   Heat 1 tablespoon of the oil in a large skillet over medium heat. Add the shallot and jalapeño and cook until the shallot is translucent and just starting to get a bit golden, 5 to 6 minutes.

2   Carefully transfer the cooked jalapeño and shallot to a large bowl. Set the pan aside; you will use it again to cook the burgers. Add the corn, beans, Old Bay, cumin, garlic powder, and paprika. Mash with a fork until around half the beans are totally smooth. For best results, it's worth taking a little taste before you add the egg to see if the mixture needs any extra salt.

3   Mix in the egg, then add the panko slowly, mixing until the mixture feels like it will hold together when pressed into patties. If it feels wet and slippery, add more panko or crush the black beans more.

4   Form the mixture into 4 patties with your hands. Put the same skillet back on the heat over medium-low and add the remaining tablespoon of oil. Once the oil is hot, add the patties and cook until golden brown, 3 to 5 minutes per side.

Smarter Tip

✳ These are great served with spicy mayo—just mix mayo with your favorite hot sauce to taste! I'm not a big buns guy, so I usually have these just with sauce, but most people like them made up on brioche.

Mom's Lentils

MAKES 3 OR 4 SERVINGS

2 tablespoons extra-virgin olive oil

3 carrots, diced

1 shallot, minced

1 head bok choy, chopped (optional)

2 garlic cloves, chopped or minced

1 cup green or French lentils, washed and drained

2 to 3 cups vegetable stock or water

½ teaspoon ground cumin

Kosher salt and freshly ground black pepper to taste

I like lentils and rice just as much as I like rice and beans, but lentils take a lot less time to cook, and you don't need to soak them before cooking.

Heat the oil in a medium pot over medium heat. Add the carrots, shallot, bok choy, and garlic and cook until aromatic. Add the lentils and enough stock or water so that the liquid fully covers the lentils.

Add the cumin and season with salt and pepper. Bring the mixture to a boil, lower the heat to a simmer, and cook until the lentils are soft, about 20 minutes.

Smarter Tip

✳ Serve these over rice, with a yogurt sauce (see one easy recipe on page 107) and a fried egg on top.

Proteins

To grow big and strong

A Note on Oven Temperature

According to *Cook's Illustrated,*[14] home ovens can vary by as much as 90°F when set to the same temperature. There is an illusion that the numbers you set are exact, but it is more likely than not that your oven either runs hot or cold. It's a good idea to figure out how it runs with a cheap oven thermometer.

Additionally, gas and electric ovens each work differently, and convection settings also add in another variable. My preference is for an electric oven with convection capability.

What is convection? You've probably heard that "heat rises," but might not have known why. Broadly speaking, convection is the transfer of energy through circulation of heat in gas or liquid. It occurs in nature, affecting systems like wind and ocean currents. Warm liquid and gas have less dense particles that rise; meanwhile cooler particles are held closer together and fall down. This bi-directional motion creates a cyclical current.

While convection is always occurring, an oven fan can force them to go faster. Circulating air inside the oven cooks food more efficiently. "True European convection" ovens include an additional heating element behind the oven fan to keep the circulating air extra warm.

Practically speaking, you should remember that convection settings make the oven temperature "feel like" it's about 25°F hotter than a standard oven.

This means if you're using a recipe written for 350°F but you decide to use convection, you may want to adjust down to 325°F. Some ovens automatically compensate for this; for example, if you type in 425°F on convection mode, it autocorrects to 400°F.

For clarity, in the recipes in which I prefer convection, I'll give you temperatures with and without it.

Lemon and Parsley

Parsley gets a lot of undeserved flak. A lot of times it's framed as an afterthought or a last-ditch attempt to make something look a little less monotone. This is a sentiment with which I vehemently disagree. In my book, parsley and lemon are a power couple. Parsley offers a very neutral but pleasant freshness, which many dishes are BEGGING for, especially after braising, stewing, or frying. When paired with a squeeze of fresh lemon, parsley can take hundreds of dishes to the next level. It adds dimension to what might be an otherwise flat dish. I guess the Italians kept this in mind when they invented the gremolata, a condiment made up of mainly lemon zest and parsley.

As iconic as they are, lemon and parsley don't always match up to the flavor profile of every dish. They work well with most European and Middle Eastern dishes, but sometimes you need to employ their alter ego, cilantro and lime, which tends to pair well with Latin American and Southeast Asian dishes.

And while you're the boss in your own kitchen, to me, the idea of putting (yellow) lemon juice on a taco feels almost as sacrilegious as using olive oil in teriyaki salmon. Giving a bit of thought to what staples are traditionally used in a particular cuisine will improve the taste and quality of your dishes.

Flavorful Braising (for Red Meat)

If you zoom out completely, braising is a two-step cooking technique: first you sear meat on high heat to get color on the outside, and then you simmer it, lid on, in a flavorful liquid until tender. You can also braise fish, vegetables, and chicken, but the time scales are a bit different, so here I'm just focusing on red meats.

Historically, braising was a way for poor people to make cheap cuts of meat with lots of fat and connective tissue palatable, since those cuts require a long cooking time to break them down and make them tender.[15]

When you first sear the meat, the only goal is to get browning on each side. You do not have to worry at all about actually cooking the meat through. When cooking in the flavorful liquid, the meat should not be fully submerged; between ½ and 1 inch should pop out over the liquid. You can either simmer the meat on the stove over low heat or opt for a more hands-off approach in the oven at a low temperature (usually between 275°F and 325°F).

Some examples of braising cuts are chuck roast, short ribs, brisket, beef cheek, stew meat, pork butt, pork shoulder, lamb shank, and oxtail.

I prefer a dutch oven that is relatively wide and not too tall, because it helps get a better sear. You could also sear the meat and start the sauce in a cast-iron pan, then switch to a pot for the actual braising if you are worried about your pot being too tall. The reason a tall pot can disrupt a good sear is that the walls obstruct airflow and create extra steam, whereas you need the meat to stay drier to get good color.

Here are the stages I use for a flavorful braise:

1. **Sear your salted meat.** You may want to use some neutral oil to help with the searing, but some of these cuts have a lot of fat on them to begin with, so it is not always necessary to use oil. Depending on how much meat you are using, you may need to sear it in batches. It is more important to develop deep color than it is to get it all done in one step. You want to use very high heat and not rush it. Unless you are burning the meat (which you don't want), it's otherwise difficult to overdo the sear. Once the meat has a deep golden-brown color, you can set it aside on a plate for later.

2. **Get your aromatics going.** After the meat has been seared and set aside, I typically add onions to the same pan. Onions are a staple ingredient in my kitchen, but they aren't your only option. Leeks, for example, are great in this step too. I like to cut fairly large pieces of onion, because the braise goes for several hours, and I want them to keep some structural integrity, rather than turn into mush. This is very much a personal preference, however, and if you don't love the appearance of onion chunks in your final

dish, you may choose to cut them thin. It'll be great either way. Your onions (or shallots or leeks) will also help lift up all the flavorful brown bits (called the fond) from the bottom of the pan.

3. **Add ingredients that require toasting or caramelization.** A lot of ingredients benefit immensely from toasting or caramelization. Some that I typically use in my braises are tomato paste, dried herbs and spices, and even flour, which works as a thickening agent for the sauce. (Flour can be omitted to keep it gluten-free.) Letting these ingredients cook before adding the liquid significantly improves the flavor of the final dish. If you added the tomato paste and flour directly to the liquid, instead of to the dry pan (with the onions), you would get a sort of gummy-raw taste, even after simmering for hours. And frying up the spices, even something as basic as black pepper, gets you a lot more flavor. I like to start with tomato paste and let it cook with the onions for up to 10 minutes over medium heat. While that is cooking, it's a good time to clean and cut celery and carrots, which don't need prior cooking to impart their best flavor. After the tomato paste has had plenty of time to develop a richer flavor (you will notice its color darkening), I typically add about 2 tablespoons of all-purpose flour along with any dried spices I'm using. This is also a good time to add fresh garlic. You can sprinkle it directly on top of the onion–tomato paste mixture, and then I like to cook that for an additional 4 to 6 minutes. Again, I do not want to taste raw flour!

4. **Add in carrots and celery, then the seared meat on top.** Alternatively you can add the carrots later, along with the potatoes, if you prefer your carrots firmer.

5. **Add in flavorful liquids.** Once you add your liquid, there is no going back! Before adding it, it's really important to make sure there's no other ingredient that needs to be toasted or caramelized. The liquids are where you can get really creative; just make sure to not add too much. You want the liquid level to *not quite* cover the meat. I typically use a base of red wine and broth, but there is a lot of room to experiment. You want to hit all the tasting notes, especially acidity and sweetness. Those will help balance out the savoriness of the meat. Some other things I might add in for good measure include fruit preserves, especially apricot or fig, pomegranate molasses, a dash of soy sauce or shio koji, a heaping spoonful of white miso (not quite a liquid), Calabrian chili bomba paste, Coca-Cola . . .

6. **Simmer for a long time.** Usually the minimum is 3 hours for red meat, but some cuts can benefit from cooking even

Flavorful Braising (*continued*)

up to 8 hours! You can put the whole pot (covered) in an oven set to 300°F, or simmer on the stove if you are confident in your ability to maintain a low heat.

7. **Add in potatoes (if using) 1 hour before you're done.** Potatoes soaked in delicious sauce is one of the best parts of braising meat. But if you cook them for, say, 5 hours (or more!), they're going to turn into mush and you won't be able to enjoy them.

8. **Deal with accumulated fat.** Braising cuts of meat have a lot of fat in them, which they will render out while cooking. The fat will mostly float and pool at the top. I find that it detracts from the flavor of the braising liquid, so I try to skim off as much as possible. If you want to get really precise, the best way to remove the fat is to put the whole pot in the fridge overnight and let the fat solidify, or use a gravy separator if you have one. If you're not in a rush, braises almost always taste better the next day, and you can also use this as a strategy to stagger your food prep if you are hosting people.

Extra Credit

✳ You can strain out the meat and vegetables from the braising liquid, chill the liquid, separate and discard the fat, then reduce the braising liquid by simmering for 10 to 15 minutes. This will make an extra-fancy sauce. Taste it and see what it needs; often a little wine or apple cider vinegar goes a long way. Finally, with the sauce at a very low simmer, mix in 2 tablespoons of cold butter to make it super luxe.

Coca-Cola Braised Brisket

DAIRY-FREE
GLUTEN-FREE OPTION ... Omit the flour

MAKES 4 TO 6 SERVINGS

For the meat

4 to 6 pounds flat (first cut) brisket (you can also use chuck roast or short ribs); see Flavorful Braising on page 116 for more

2 tablespoons kosher salt

2 tablespoons neutral oil

For the aromatics

5 shallots, cut into thick slices

6 ounces shiitake mushrooms, roughly chopped

2 tablespoons all-purpose flour

2 tablespoons tomato paste

1 teaspoon freshly ground black pepper

2 celery stalks, thinly sliced

1 teaspoon Szeged sweet paprika

1 teaspoon garlic powder

For the liquid

1 (12-ounce) can Coca-Cola (regular)

2 cups beef or chicken stock (you can also use water and bouillon)

1 (14-ounce) can whole peeled San Marzano tomatoes

1 tablespoon Calabrian chili bomba paste

Finishing touches

5 or 6 carrots, split down the middle

1 pound small yellow potatoes, halved

1 bunch fresh parsley, chopped

Possible sauce adjustments

½ cup Coca-Cola

1 cup beef or chicken stock (you can also use water and bouillon)

1 teaspoon potato starch

Kosher salt to taste

1 to 2 tablespoons apple cider vinegar

As I explained in my section on Flavorful Braising (page 116), these sorts of recipes offer lots of room for creativity. This recipe and Engagement Short Ribs (page 122) demonstrate some of the range of flavors you can get with what is essentially the same method.

While most spices benefit from a few minutes of frying in oil to "bloom" the flavor, garlic powder and paprika are very fine powders with more of an affinity to burn than, say, black pepper and oregano. So while heating them will definitely wake them up, I prefer to add them right before the liquid.

This entire dish can be made the day ahead, and it can actually be easier to do it that way (and the flavor will be even better).

1 Prep the meat: Sprinkle the meat with 1 tablespoon of the salt. You can do this ahead, up to overnight (place the meat in the fridge), or just 10 to 15 minutes before searing.

2 Sear the meat: Heat a large dutch oven over high heat for 2 minutes and then add the oil. Once you add the oil, let it heat up for 1 more minute before adding the meat. Brisket can be too big to lay flat in the dutch oven, so you may need to get creative with your tongs to get a good sear. (Alternatively, you can sear the meat in a wider skillet and use that until step 6. Then, deglaze with the Coca-Cola, pour everything into the dutch oven, and continue.) Sear the meat on all sides, until it develops a deep golden-brown color and the fatty parts on the outside are golden and starting to render. It can be helpful to press the meat into the pan with tongs to

RECIPE CONTINUES

make sure it's in good contact with the pan. It's hard to overdo this step (unless you're burning the meat), so take your time to make sure everything is well seared on all sides. Once you're happy with the sear, remove the meat and set it aside on a plate for later. You may need as much as 5 to 7 minutes per side to get a deep enough color.

3   Preheat the oven to 300°F.

4   **Make the aromatics aromatic:** Lower the heat to medium-low. Add the shallots and mushrooms and stir. Let them cook for 2 to 3 minutes and get a little bit of color, then add the flour, tomato paste, and pepper. Cook for 5 to 7 more minutes, stirring often, until the flour and tomato paste have had time to lose their raw edge. Add the celery, paprika, and garlic powder.

5   **Start the sauce:** Add the Coca-Cola, stock, tomatoes, and chili paste. Bring to a boil and stir, then turn off the heat.

6   **Get ready for the oven:** Add the meat back into the pan (along with any accumulated juices on the plate). Pour in enough water (if needed; you may not need any) so that the meat is mostly submerged in the liquid, with about ½ inch sticking out above the liquid line.

Cover the pot and place in the oven for about 4 hours, undisturbed.

7   **Add in the veg:** At the 4-hour mark, add the carrots and potatoes on top of the meat, cover, and cook until the carrots and potatoes are cooked through and the meat is fork-tender, 1 more hour.

8   **Make it fancy:** *To take this dish up a notch, you can reduce the braising liquid into a luxurious sauce. To start this process, the first step is to separate the meat and veggies from the sauce.*

9   Once the potatoes and carrots are tender, use a sieve to strain the braising liquid into a freezer-safe container. Transfer the meat and vegetables to an oven-safe serving vessel (I like to use something that works well in the fridge and oven).

10   **If serving the same day:** Cover the meat and veggies with aluminum foil and place in the oven at 200°F. The meat and vegetables will stay good all day at that temperature until you are ready to serve. Place the strained braising liquid (your future sauce) in the freezer—this will solidify the fat, which will float to the top so you can scrape it off. If you have a gravy separator, you can use that instead of freezing it. Once the fat does solidify (it'll form an orangey

layer at the top), use a metal spoon to scrape it off and discard.

11   If it looks like there won't be a good amount of sauce, you can add more Coca-Cola and stock to the strained liquid.

12   Then, place the sauce into a saucepan and simmer over medium heat for 10 minutes. The sauce will get a bit thicker, but if it feels super thin, you can mix the potato starch in just enough water to dissolve it, then add it to the simmering sauce.

13   Taste for salt and adjust as needed. You may want to add a tablespoon or two of apple cider vinegar to brighten up the sauce (if needed). Right before serving, top the meat and veggies with the parsley.

14   **If serving the next day (easier):** Cover the meat and veggies with aluminum foil and place in the refrigerator. Cover the braising liquid and refrigerate it overnight. One hour before serving, place the meat and veggies in the oven at 200°F to reheat. They can stay at that temperature for several hours, as needed. Use a spoon to scrape the congealed fat off the braising liquid and discard the fat. Finish cooking the sauce as described above.

Engagement Short Ribs

MAKES 2 TO 3 SERVINGS

DAIRY-FREE
GLUTEN-FREE OPTION ... Omit the flour; use tamari or gluten-free soy sauce and gluten-free miso

For the meat

3 to 4 short ribs (English cut, not flanken); or use brisket or chuck; see Flavorful Braising on page 116 for more

1 tablespoon kosher salt, plus more to taste

2 tablespoons neutral oil

For the aromatics

1 onion, cut into thick slices

1 leek, thinly sliced (optional)

10 garlic cloves, whole but peeled

2 tablespoons all-purpose flour

½ teaspoon red pepper flakes

1 teaspoon herbes de Provence

1 teaspoon freshly ground black pepper

2 celery stalks, thinly sliced

For the liquid

2 cups red wine

½ cup dried cranberries

¼ cup apricot jam

¼ cup white miso

2 tablespoons soy sauce

1 teaspoon bouillon paste

1 sprig fresh rosemary

Finishing touches

5 or 6 carrots, split down the middle

1 pound small yellow potatoes, halved

1 to 2 tablespoons apple cider vinegar (if needed)

1 bunch fresh parsley, chopped

If they are The One, no amount of garlic should deter them.

Given the fact that I am single at the time of writing this, I can't necessarily claim that they will say yes after trying this dish and you'll live happily ever after . . . but what I can say is that if I wanted to propose to someone, this dish would be at the top of my agenda.

While this recipe takes many hours to complete, the vast majority of the cook time is inactive, and the short ribs will be just chillin' (well, actually the opposite of that) in the oven for 5 to 6 hours, while you are able to do whatever you want around the house. And this is a dish with built-in sides, so the wait is definitely worth it. I like to add in the potatoes and carrots toward the end so they keep their structural integrity.

Even though this dish has a very Western flavor profile, miso and soy sauce add savoriness and depth of flavor.

This entire dish can be made the day ahead, and it can actually be easier to do it that way (and the flavor will be even better).

1 **Prep the meat:** Sprinkle the meat with 1 tablespoon of the salt. You can do this ahead, up to overnight (place the meat in the fridge), or just 10 to 15 minutes before searing.

2 **Sear the meat:** Heat a large dutch oven over high heat for 2 minutes and then add the oil. Once you add the oil, let it heat up for 1 more minute before adding the meat. Do not crowd the pan, so if you don't have enough surface area to easily brown the meat all at once, do it in batches. Pat the meat dry, then sear the meat on all sides, until the meat develops a deep golden-brown color and the fatty parts on the outside are golden and starting to render. It can be helpful to press the meat into the pan with tongs to make sure it's making good contact with the pan. It's hard to overdo this step (unless you're burning the meat), so take your time to make sure everything is well seared on all sides. Once you're happy with the sear, remove the meat and set it aside on a plate for later.

3 Preheat the oven to 300°F.

RECIPE CONTINUES

4 Make the aromatics aromatic:
Lower the heat to medium-low. Add the onion and the leek (if using) and stir. Cook until they get a little bit of color, 2 to 3 minutes, then add the garlic, flour, red pepper flakes, herbes de Provence, and pepper. Cook, stirring often, until the spices are toasty and fragrant, 2 to 3 more minutes.

5 Start the sauce: Add the celery, then mix in the wine, dried cranberries, apricot jam, miso, soy sauce, and bouillon paste. Bring to a boil and stir, then turn off the heat.

6 Get ready for the oven: Add the meat back into the pan (along with any accumulated juices on the plate). Pour in enough water (if needed; you may not need any) so that the meat is mostly submerged in the liquid, with about ½ inch sticking out above the liquid line. Top with the rosemary. Cover the pot and place in the oven for 4½ hours, undisturbed.

7 Add in the veg: At the 4½-hour mark, place the carrots and potatoes on top of the meat, cover, and cook for 1½ hours more.

8 Make it fancy: *To take this dish up a notch, you can reduce the braising liquid into a luxurious sauce. To start this process, the first step is to separate the meat and veggies from the sauce.*

9 Once the potatoes and carrots are tender, use a sieve to strain the braising liquid into a freezer-safe container. Transfer the meat and vegetables to an oven-safe serving vessel (I like to use something that works well in the fridge and oven).

10 If serving the same day:
Cover the meat and veggies with aluminum foil and place in the oven at 200°F. The meat and vegetables will stay good all day at that temperature until you are ready to serve. Place the strained braising liquid (your future sauce) in the freezer—this will quickly solidify the fat, which will float to the top so you can scrape it off. If you have a gravy separator, you can use that instead of freezing it. Once the fat does solidify (it'll form an orangey layer at the top), use a metal spoon to scrape it off and discard.

11 Then, place the remaining sauce into a saucepan and simmer for

10 minutes. The sauce will get a bit thicker. Taste for salt and adjust as needed. You may want to add a tablespoon or two of apple cider vinegar to brighten up the sauce (if needed). Right before serving, top the meat and veggies with the parsley.

12 If serving the next day (easier):
Cover the meat and veggies with aluminum foil and place in the refrigerator. Cover the braising liquid and also refrigerate it overnight. One hour before serving the next day, place the meat and veggies in the oven at 200°F to reheat. They can stay at that temperature for several hours, as needed. Use a spoon to scrape the congealed fat off the braising liquid and discard the fat. Finish cooking the sauce as described above.

Marinades

These marinades are versatile and can be used with a variety of proteins. I've included some pictures to show you serving suggestions, but I challenge you to get creative.

For all of these marinades: Mix the ingredients in a ziplock bag. (Or, to marinate without using any plastic, place the marinade and protein in a bowl and simply cover with a plate.) Marinate overnight or as instructed in the recipe. Roast or grill as desired.

All-Purpose Yogurt Marinade

GREAT FOR BONELESS CHICKEN
VEGETARIAN
GLUTEN-FREE

ALL STAPLE INGREDIENTS

1 cup whole milk Greek yogurt

2 garlic cloves, chopped

1 teaspoon sweet paprika

1 teaspoon ground cumin

1 teaspoon red pepper flakes

¼ teaspoon ground cinnamon

Zest and juice of 1 lemon

2 teaspoons kosher salt

1 teaspoon freshly ground black pepper

Sweet Chili Miso Marinade

GREAT WITH SALMON
VEGAN
VEGETARIAN
DAIRY-FREE
GLUTEN-FREE OPTION ... Use tamari or gluten-free soy sauce and gluten-free miso

ALL STAPLE INGREDIENTS

⅓ cup white miso

½ cup sweet chili sauce

2 tablespoons soy sauce

½ cup unseasoned rice wine vinegar

3 bird's eye (Thai) chilies, sliced

1 shallot, minced

2 tablespoons sesame seeds

Spicy Za'atar Marinade

GOOD FOR CHICKEN: WHOLE, SPATCHCOCKED, OR BONELESS
VEGETARIAN
GLUTEN-FREE

ALL STAPLE INGREDIENTS

1 teaspoon kosher salt

1 shallot, minced

2 dates, pitted and chopped

3 garlic cloves, crushed

2 tablespoons extra-virgin olive oil

Freshly ground black pepper to taste

½ cup whole milk Greek yogurt

2 tablespoons za'atar

2 teaspoons ground cumin

½ teaspoon sweet paprika

1 tablespoon Calabrian chili bomba paste

¼ teaspoon red pepper flakes

Juice of ½ lemon

Smarter Tip

✳ For chicken wings, preheat the oven to 400°F (375° if using convection) and line a half sheet pan with aluminum foil. Put the marinated wings on the prepared pan, leaving space between each one. Cook for 15 minutes on each side or until nicely browned and slightly crispy. Good hot or at room temperature.

Peruvian-Inspired Marinade

GREAT FOR A CUT-UP WHOLE CHICKEN
AND CHICKEN WINGS
VEGAN
VEGETARIAN
DAIRY-FREE
GLUTEN-FREE

1 tablespoon dried oregano

¼ cup packed brown sugar

1 teaspoon sweet paprika

4 garlic cloves, chopped

1 teaspoon chili powder

½ teaspoon ground cumin

Kosher salt and freshly ground black
    pepper to taste

Juice of 3 limes

Mom's Favorite Marinade

GREAT FOR CHICKEN WINGS AND SALMON
VEGAN
VEGETARIAN
DAIRY-FREE
GLUTEN-FREE OPTION... Use tamari or gluten-free
soy sauce

ALL STAPLE INGREDIENTS

½ cup soy sauce

¼ cup packed brown sugar

Juice of 3 limes

1 tablespoon dried oregano

2 teaspoons sweet paprika

1 teaspoon ginger (ground or minced
    fresh)

Smarter Tip

* My mom often makes her Favorite
  Marinade and splits it between
  chicken and salmon, so she can
  grill them both at the same time
  and people can choose their
  preference.

Peruvian-Inspired Marinade (page 127)

All-Purpose Yogurt Marinade (page 126)

Mom's Favorite Marinade (page 127)

Apricot-Glazed Chicken

DAIRY-FREE
GLUTEN-FREE

MAKES 3 TO 4 SERVINGS

USE CONVECTION IF YOU HAVE IT

For the chicken and aromatics

8 bone-in, skin-on chicken thighs

3 teaspoons kosher salt

⅔ cup (4 ounces/120g) dried apricots (about 15)

1 red onion, sliced into thick wedges

1 teaspoon freshly ground black pepper

½ cup dry white wine

½ cup chicken stock

For the glaze

1 teaspoon sweet paprika

½ teaspoon red pepper flakes

¼ cup apricot jam

¼ cup olive oil

1 teaspoon dijon mustard

1 tablespoon apple cider vinegar

¼ teaspoon cayenne pepper (optional)

Chopped fresh parsley, for garnish

With dried fruit, roasted chicken, and a pan sauce, this dish is a bit reminiscent of chicken marbella, which is one of my favorite childhood dishes. Unlike chicken marbella, you do not need to marinate it ahead of time. You can use chicken thighs or a cut-up whole chicken.

1   Prep the chicken: Preheat the oven to 375°F (or 350°F if using convection).

2   Arrange the chicken on a half sheet pan and season evenly with the salt. Place the apricots and onions on the pan around the chicken.

3   Make the glaze: Combine the paprika, red pepper flakes, apricot jam, olive oil, mustard, vinegar, and cayenne (if using) in a small bowl and mix with a fork. Spread the glaze over the chicken (not the apricots and onion). Season with the pepper. Put the pan into the oven, then carefully pour the wine and stock into the pan around the chicken pieces.

4   Bake for 45 to 55 minutes, until the skin is golden brown. Periodically use a spoon to move around the onions and apricots and baste the chicken with the juices. If the chicken is browning unevenly, rotate the pan as well.

5   Garnish with parsley.

Slow-Cooked Ginger Chicken

MAKES 3 TO 4 SERVINGS

DAIRY-FREE
GLUTEN-FREE OPTION ... Use tamari or gluten-free soy sauce

1 tablespoon toasted sesame oil

8 boneless skinless chicken thighs

1 tablespoon chopped fresh ginger

3 tablespoons soy sauce

2 teaspoons brown sugar

1 teaspoon apple cider vinegar

Sesame seeds, for garnish

This was a frequent dinner in our house growing up. It's very low effort—just pour everything in the pan and stick it in the oven. Serve it over rice.

1 Preheat the oven to 300°F.

2 Spread the sesame oil in the bottom of a 9 × 13-inch baking dish and then add the chicken. Combine the ginger, soy sauce, brown sugar, and apple cider vinegar in a small bowl. Pour the sauce over the chicken.

3 Place the chicken in the oven and bake, uncovered, for about 30 minutes, until slightly browned on top. Flip the chicken over and bake, uncovered, for another 30 minutes. Cover and bake for another hour, until very tender and the chicken pulls apart easily with a fork. Use two forks to shred the chicken, if desired. Sprinkle with sesame seeds.

Chicken Thighs with Date Butter Sauce

GLUTEN-FREE

USE CONVECTION IF YOU HAVE IT

MAKES 3 TO 4 SERVINGS

8 tablespoons (1 stick) unsalted butter, softened

2 teaspoons kosher salt

1 teaspoon freshly ground black pepper

1 teaspoon red pepper flakes

8 bone-in, skin-on chicken thighs

8 dates, pitted and thinly sliced

8 carrots, chopped

1 celery stalk, thinly sliced

½ red onion, sliced into rings

½ cup dry white wine (or enough to coat the pan evenly)

Juice of ½ lemon

½ cup minced parsley (optional)

Because this dish is the cover photo, it reminds me of the point in a movie where they say the name of the movie *in* the movie. Sweet dates and carrots create harmony with buttery crispy chicken skin, while red onions and celery ground this dish with freshness. White wine and lemon juice makes everything pop. I always appreciate a simple but delicious dinner that cooks veggies and protein in one dish together.

1 Preheat the oven to 400°F (or 375°F if using convection).

2 Mix together the butter, salt, pepper, and red pepper flakes in a medium bowl.

3 Arrange the chicken evenly on a half sheet pan. Rub the butter mixture onto the skin. Place the dates, carrots, celery, and red onions in the pan around the chicken.

4 Place the pan in the oven, then carefully pull out the rack and pour the wine around the chicken. Bake for 40 to 45 minutes, until the skin is crispy. Finish the chicken with a squeeze of lemon juice.

Honey Lemon Chicken

MAKES 2 TO 3 SERVINGS

2 chicken breasts or equivalent chicken cutlets or chicken tenders (you can cut them how you like, but I like them pounded and cut into thin strips)

Kosher salt and freshly ground black pepper

½ cup all-purpose flour, for dredging

1 teaspoon garlic powder

1 teaspoon Szeged sweet paprika

Dried oregano (optional)

2 tablespoons extra-virgin olive oil

2 tablespoons unsalted butter

½ cup chicken stock

2 tablespoons honey

3 lemons

Red pepper flakes (optional)

Finely chopped fresh parsley, for garnish

This is a very popular recipe with my family when I am home. It is also easy enough that two of my brothers, Leo and Gabriel, make it when they have guests over. We often dredge the chicken in just well-seasoned flour, but Mom also frequently adds a coating of beaten egg and panko bread crumbs for more crunch. The beauty of this recipe is that you can use the same process—searing the chicken on the stove, then cooking it in the oven with a flavorful sauce—with just about any flavor combination. For a twist, use lime instead of lemon, add sautéed peppers and onions, cumin, and chili powder. Serve the chicken over rice.

1   Preheat the oven to 375°F.

2   Season the chicken with salt and pepper. Combine the flour, garlic powder, paprika, and oregano (if using) in a shallow bowl or a plate with a raised edge.

3   Heat a large skillet over medium heat, then add the oil. The pan should be hot enough that the chicken sizzles.

4   Work in batches if necessary to avoid crowding the pan. Lightly coat the chicken pieces in the seasoned flour, shake off the excess, and add the chicken to the pan along with 1 tablespoon of the butter. You aren't trying to fully cook the chicken at this point, just to get color on it, which will take 3 to 4 minutes on each side.

5   Transfer the browned chicken to an oven-safe dish. Add the remaining tablespoon butter, the chicken stock, and the honey to the same pan that you cooked the chicken in. Let the mixture simmer briefly, then pour the sauce over the chicken in the dish. Squeeze the juice of 1 to 2 lemons over the chicken.

6   Cut the third lemon into thin slices (remove the seeds; they will make it bitter!) and arrange them in the dish with the chicken. Top with red pepper flakes if desired.

7   Bake for 25 to 30 minutes, until the chicken is deeply golden brown, the sauce is a bit thicker, and the lemons are softened and slightly caramelized (you can eat them!).

8   Top with parsley and serve.

Deeper Dive: A few tips for making the perfect honey lemon chicken

* Don't skimp on the seasoning. Feel free to add more.

* Make sure the pan is hot to get good color on the chicken.

* It's important not to crowd the chicken pieces so that they brown properly. You can cook them in batches if they don't all fit comfortably in the pan.

* Make some rice (and a veggie) while the chicken is in the oven!

* The oven is used mainly to cook the chicken all the way through and to get a little caramelization on the lemons; plus it gives you time to clean up and prepare other parts of the meal.

Jewish Mother Chicken Soup

MAKES 4 TO 6 SERVINGS

DAIRY-FREE
GLUTEN-FREE OPTION ... Omit the noodles or matzo balls, substitute rice, or use gluten-free noodles

1 whole raw chicken plus 1 pound additional bony chicken parts, such as legs, wings, necks, and backs

1 large yellow onion

1 pound carrots

½ bunch celery

1 pound parsnips

1 thumb-size piece of ginger

1 sweet potato (optional)

1 bunch fresh parsley (optional)

Kosher salt

Cooked egg noodles or matzo balls, for serving (optional)

Dill, for serving (optional)

You can learn a lot about someone based on how they make their chicken soup. If they don't use parsnips, I don't trust them. Just saying . . . Not only is this matzo ball soup (or chicken noodle) delicious, it's straight-up medicine. When you or a friend is feeling under the weather, you should definitely have this recipe up your sleeve. You're pretty much just dumping a bunch of stuff in a stockpot and letting it simmer for a couple hours; it's so easy to make!

Even though there are only 10 to 20 minutes of active work, you do need to be home for at least 3 hours to monitor the stove, so I recommend picking a day when you have a lot of stuff to do at home (even if it's just binge-watching Netflix). Once the soup is made, you can freeze it for a few months or keep it in the fridge for up to a week. You can eat it as is or incorporate your homemade broth in other recipes.

1   Place the chicken pieces in a large stockpot. Fill the pot with cold water, enough to cover all the eventual ingredients. Set the pot on medium-high heat while you prep the vegetables. As you prep each vegetable, add it to the pot and move on to the next: Wash and halve the onion, leaving the skin on. Scrub, trim, and halve the carrots lengthwise. Trim and halve the celery crosswise. Wash, trim, and halve the parsnips lengthwise. Wash and halve the ginger. Wash and halve the sweet potato (if using). Add the parsley.

2   Bring to a boil uncovered, then reduce to a simmer, cover, and let simmer for 3 to 6 hours. After an hour or two, crack the lid a little to allow the soup to concentrate as it simmers. The soup can be done after 3 hours, but the flavor will continue to improve the longer you go. Skim and discard any scum that floats to the top as it boils. Turn off the heat. If you have time to spare, you can let the soup sit on the stove for 30 minutes to an hour with the heat off. Otherwise, continue but be careful; it will be very hot.

3   In the sink, prepare a metal colander or large sieve over a very large bowl or a second, slightly smaller pot. Strain the soup through the colander into the second bowl or pot. (Try to pour the broth out on its own and keep the chicken in the original

RECIPE CONTINUES

pot without plopping it into the colander.)

4 Use a fork to pick out the chicken meat from the skin and bones. Store in a separate airtight container. If desired, remove the cooked carrots from the colander and store them in another airtight container. Thank the rest of the ingredients for their service and discard them.

5 Salt the broth generously to taste (it will need a lot), and serve immediately as a broth with noodles or matzo balls (if desired), the reserved chicken and carrots, and dill (if desired). To store in the fridge, divide the broth into smaller shallow containers. Best food-safety practice (see page xxix) is actually to put it in the fridge while it's still warm, as long as it's not in one huge container. When kept in the fridge, your homemade broth will congeal. This is normal, desirable, and an indication of a well-made broth. The gelatin texture will melt as soon as the soup is reheated.

6 **For extra freshness:** *Slice new carrots and celery and simmer them for 10 minutes in the stock before serving.*

Smarter Tips

✳ You can be flexible with the bones or parts that you use. If you are using chicken parts for other purposes, it's usually cheaper to buy a whole chicken than a cut-up one. You can butcher it yourself or even take the whole chicken package to the butcher counter at your grocery store; they'll do it for free. Then save and freeze the carcasses to make this broth. Two carcasses with some additional legs is a great way to do this.

✳ Some people prefer to remove the chicken off the bones around the 1 hour mark, for a springier texture—putting the bones but not the meat back in for the rest of the cook time. I do not mind the texture of the meat when cooked the whole way through; it's more shredded.

✳ You can also freeze veggie scraps from cooking on an ongoing basis; store them in an airtight freezer bag or container and save them to add to the soup as well.

✳ Any bone broth will naturally create some scum when it boils. You'll want to scrape off and strain out those impurities. However, it can be beneficial to discard the whole first pot of water after the bones and veggies initially come to a boil. At this point, I like to rinse everything a few times with fresh cold water and get out anything that might still be stuck on the veggies. Then refill with fresh water and bring back to a boil before starting the multi-hour simmer-sesh. It'll make for a much cleaner broth and there will be less scum to scrape off as the cooking goes on.

Aunt Rachel's Infinitely Adaptable Ginger Chicken Soup

DAIRY-FREE
GLUTEN-FREE

MAKES 3 TO 5 SERVINGS

3 bone-in chicken breasts, skin removed, plus (optional) 2 boneless, skinless chicken thighs for extra heartiness

1 to 2 heaping tablespoons kosher salt (to taste)

1 hand-size piece fresh ginger (look for shiny skin for best freshness)

8 to 10 garlic cloves

2 to 3 carrots

1 onion

5 to 10 whole peppercorns (take them out of your pepper grinder)

1 small sweet potato (optional)

1 to 2 celery stalks (optional)

Okay, infinite adaptations might be an exaggeration. But I confirmed with my uncle Jason, who is an engineer, and with my aunt Rachel's list of adaptations (page 145), a conservative estimate would give 32,767 ways you can customize this soup. For those of you who aren't familiar with my poor math skills, you should be very impressed right now; I had to use, like, Pascal's triangle.

And if 32,000 possible dinners isn't enough excitement for you (it is for me), as a by-product of making your own quick chicken broth, you are also left with beautiful poached chicken breasts, which you can serve in the finished soup or use to add protein to a number of dishes throughout the week: in wraps, sandwiches, or salads. So if you ask me, the limit does not exist. This is really the ultimate meal-prep recipe.

1   Place the chicken breasts (and thighs, if using) in a large pot and add enough water just to cover the chicken but not so much that the broth will be weak. Add the salt and set over medium-high heat as you prep the vegetables. As you prep each vegetable, add it to the pot and move on to the next: Wash and slice the ginger. Peel the garlic; leave the cloves whole or crush them for stronger flavor. Halve the carrots lengthwise. (While she's at it, Aunt Rachel cuts up extra carrots to put in the fridge as a ready-to-go snack for later.) Quarter the onion, leaving the skin on.

2   Bring the soup to a boil. If you are using the sweet potato, wash and quarter it; if using the celery, trim and halve it crosswise; add either or both to the pot.

3   Once the soup reaches a boil, reduce to a simmer and cover with the lid slightly propped to allow some steam to escape. Simmer on low heat for 30 to 40 minutes while you relax, clean up, and prep mix-ins if you're planning to serve the soup immediately.

4   After 30 minutes or so, taste the broth for depth of flavor. It will be paler than the average chicken noodle soup but should have a lot

RECIPE CONTINUES

of flavor. Add more salt if desired, but keep in mind that if you will be adding soy sauce or miso paste to the broth (see the Serving Suggestions), those ingredients bring their own salt.

5 Remove the chicken and set it aside, then strain the soup into a bowl to remove the vegetables.

(For anything you don't use immediately, let it cool slightly before storing in an airtight container in the fridge for up to a week.)

6 Shred the chicken. Add it back to the soup to serve, or save it for another use (it's good for chicken salad).

SEE PHOTO ON NEXT SPREAD

Serving Suggestions

**My aunt Rachel once said, "May your soup be tasty," and I live by that mantra.
Here are some suggested customizations to mix and match in the finished soup:**

✳ 1 portion plain ramen, udon, or other Asian noodles, cooked according to package instructions

✳ 1 to 2 tablespoons soy sauce, added to the broth

✳ Uncle David's way: a squeeze of sriracha, hoisin, fresh lime juice, and basil (it reminds him of pho)

✳ Aunt Rachel's way: Sliced shiitake mushrooms (stems removed), bok choy, sliced snow peas, and onion quickly sautéed in sesame or chili oil with a splash of soy sauce and mirin

✳ Sliced raw carrots, bok choy, and scallions, cooked in the broth

✳ Thinly sliced jalapeños or other fresh chilies

✳ Prepared dumplings (cooked according to the package instructions)

✳ Shichimi togarashi seasoning

✳ Dried seaweed snacks

✳ Thinly sliced napa cabbage, cooked in the broth, and sriracha

✳ 1 to 2 tablespoons white miso (to taste), stirred into the broth

A few notes on serving and mix-ins:

✳ Because this soup starts with a general East Asian flavor profile, you can take it in many different directions depending on what you add. You could even keep the broth base plain and add customizations by the serving, to order.

✳ My favorite way reminds me of a rich Chinese-style wonton soup: adding a dash of soy sauce and sliced scallions. You can't go wrong with a squeeze of sriracha in there either.

✳ Dissolving 1 to 2 tablespoons of white miso makes it taste like it came from your favorite Japanese spot. It's easier to mix in the paste when you simmer the stock in a small saucepan.

✳ No matter what you do, play around with herbs and seasonings and enjoy!

Roast Chicken

Roasting a chicken is one of the easiest ways to project that you have your life together, even if everything around you is in shambles. You're likely to get a fair share of oohs and aahs—enough validation to sustain me for weeks—and the gag is: you basically just turned on the oven and stuck a bird inside. No one has to know how easy it is. Let's keep it our little secret.

For good measure, you should probably rub your chicken with something flavorful, and I promise it is really easy.

There are a lot of delicious ways to dress up a chicken, such as cooking it over a bed of carrots and shallots or even some lemon slices—but at the most basic level, to me, the most important things to think about are salt and sugar.

Salt can come from a variety of sources, not just the plain crystals—for example, soy sauce, miso, fish sauce, or anchovies.

The necessity of salting your chicken is obvious to most sane people (I hope). But using sweetness as a way to balance the inherent savoriness of the meat will also make it taste incredible. My mom adds brown sugar to the spice mix of her go-to recipe. Other great options include maple syrup, honey, jam, and sweet chili sauce.

Sugars, though, whether in maple syrup or granular form, have a propensity to burn, especially at the high temperatures used to roast chicken. To get the benefits of a sweet ingredient without too much burning, I like to start a chicken in the oven at a high temperature with just salt or soy sauce, then, once the skin starts to get crispy, I lower the temperature and add a seasoned glaze or spice rub.

While they are all very similar at their core, the four roast chicken recipes in this book demonstrate a variety of techniques to take your cooking to the next level:

Mom's Roast Chicken recipe will show you how to do a spice-rubbed chicken.

Maple Butter Roast Chicken will show you how to make a compound butter.

"Soy Vay" Roast Chicken will show you that you can still roast a chicken with a wet sauce or marinade.

And the spatchcocked, yogurt-marinated Za'atar Roast Chicken will give you even more options . . .

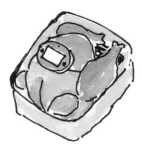

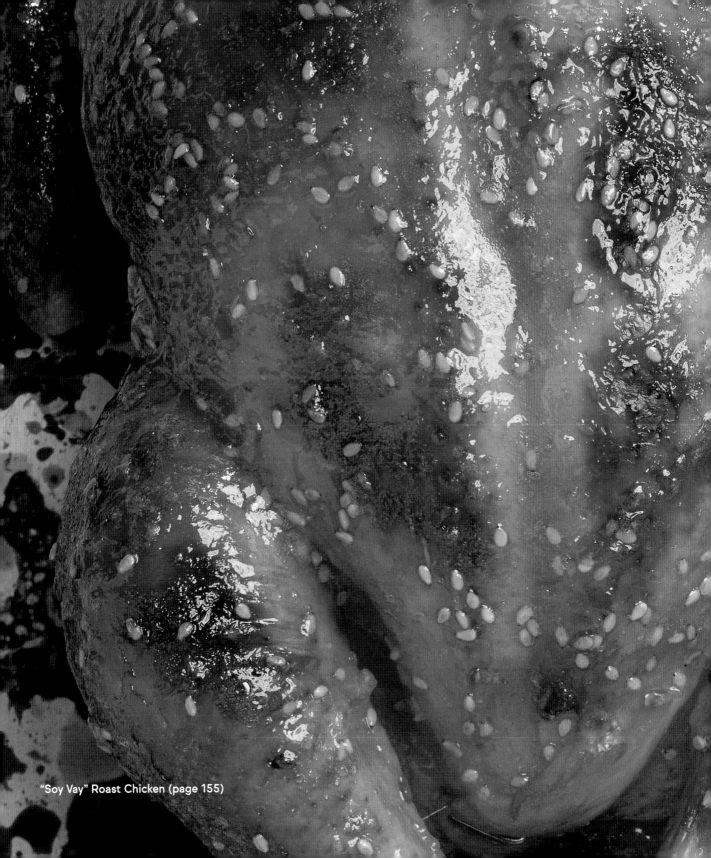
"Soy Vay" Roast Chicken (page 155)

Mom's Roast Chicken

MAKES 2 TO 4 SERVINGS

DAIRY-FREE
GLUTEN-FREE

USE CONVECTION IF YOU HAVE IT

For the chicken

1 whole chicken (remove giblets if included, pat dry, and sprinkle with kosher salt 30 minutes before starting)

1 head garlic, sliced in half

1 lemon, sliced in half (one half kept as is, the other sliced again into thin slices)

2 to 4 sprigs fresh rosemary

3 to 4 shallots, sliced

2 to 4 carrots, sliced into little strips

2 to 4 parsnips, sliced into little strips

4 to 6 tablespoons neutral oil

Spice mix

1½ teaspoons freshly ground black pepper

1 teaspoon za'atar (optional)

1 teaspoon Szeged sweet paprika

1 teaspoon garlic powder

1 teaspoon dried oregano

1 tablespoon brown sugar

2 teaspoons seasoned salt, such as Lawry's, or kosher salt

I love to serve this roast chicken with fluffy white rice so I can spoon the flavorful juices over it. Do not miss out on the caramelized lemon! The sweet, sour, and bitter tastes pair amazingly with the savory meat.

I like to use shallots in this recipe, because I find they have more flavor than onions, but you can use either.

You also don't need to tie up the chicken's legs, but if you have butcher's twine, it can help the chicken cook more evenly. You can also fold up a strip of aluminum foil and use that to bind the legs together.

The brown sugar in the rub can make the chicken look darker than it might otherwise, but it will not actually taste burned unless you REALLY overdo it. It's okay if it gets kind of dark.

1 Preheat the oven to 450°F (or 425°F if using convection).

2 Place the pre-salted chicken into a large roasting pan and pat dry. Stuff with the head of garlic, half a lemon, and 1 or 2 sprigs of the rosemary.

3 Lay the sliced shallots, lemon slices, carrots, and parsnips around the chicken.

4 Finely chop the leaves from the remaining 1 or 2 sprigs fresh rosemary. Combine the rosemary, pepper, za'atar (if using), paprika, garlic powder, oregano, brown sugar, and seasoned salt in a small bowl. Set the mix aside.

5 Roast the plain salted chicken and veggies for 15 minutes, then take the chicken out, drizzle it with enough oil to coat, and sprinkle all over with the spice mix.

6 Lower the temperature to 350°F (or 325°F if using convection) and roast for another 60 to 75 minutes, until a thermometer registers 165°F at the thickest part of the thigh (not touching the bone) or holds at 160°F for 16 seconds (see page xxviii). If you cut between the leg and the breast, the skin should be totally opaque and the juices should be clear. You may want to mix around the surrounding veggies a couple times during roasting and rotate the chicken in the oven so it cooks evenly. Let the chicken rest for about 5 minutes before serving.

KEEP GOING FOR MORE GREAT ROAST CHICKEN OPTIONS

Maple Butter Roast Chicken

MAKES 2 TO 4 SERVINGS

8 tablespoons (1 stick) unsalted butter, at room temperature

1 lemon

10 garlic cloves, roughly chopped

3 sprigs fresh rosemary (leaves removed and chopped)

Red pepper flakes to taste

Kosher salt and fresh cracked black pepper to taste

¼ cup maple syrup

1 raw whole chicken (remove giblets if included, pat dry, and *lightly* sprinkle with kosher salt 30 minutes before starting)

This roast chicken recipe uses a compound butter (a butter mixed with seasonings) to add moisture and lots of flavor. Maple, garlic, and rosemary are very classic flavors, but of course, you can season your butter with any herbs and spices you like and cook the chicken the exact same way.

1 Preheat the oven to 400°F (or 375°F if using convection).

2 Place the softened butter in a small bowl. Zest the lemon with a microplane and add the zest to the butter. Set the lemon aside. Add the garlic, rosemary, red pepper flakes, salt, and pepper. Mix the butter well, add the maple syrup, and crush up the garlic a little into the butter to help it release more flavor.

3 Pat the chicken dry again. Sprinkle with kosher salt all over to give it a *light* but even coating. Use clean hands to rub the butter mixture all over the chicken, including underneath the skin of the breast (you will need to stick your fingers between the skin and the meat to loosen it).

4 Cut the reserved lemon in half and stick it in the cavity. Use aluminum foil or butcher's twine to fasten the legs together, if desired. Roast for about 1 hour (but start checking at 45 minutes), until a thermometer registers 165°F at the thickest part of the thigh (not touching the bone) or holds at 160°F for 16 seconds (see page xxviii). If you cut between the leg and the breast, the skin should be totally opaque and the juices should be clear. The skin also usually shrivels near the legs when it's done. Let the chicken rest for about 5 minutes before serving.

"Soy Vay" Roast Chicken

MAKES 2 TO 4 SERVINGS

DAIRY-FREE
GLUTEN-FREE OPTION ... Use tamari or gluten-free soy sauce

USE CONVECTION IF YOU HAVE IT

1 whole chicken (remove giblets if included, pat dry, and sprinkle with kosher salt 30 minutes before starting)

¼ cup sweet chili sauce

3 garlic cloves, grated or minced

2 teaspoons sesame seeds

¼ cup soy sauce

Kosher salt to taste (optional)

I grew up around the corner from my grandpa Nate, and we could expect him to cook a soy roast chicken most Friday nights. I often wondered what on earth he was doing to make such a flavorful bird, but as an adult I learned that all he did was dump a bottle of Soyaki marinade on it and stick it in the oven. Soyaki (a Trader Joe's brand) and Soy Vay teriyaki sauces are basically store-bought sweet soy sauce marinades. I don't always have a bottle on hand, but I do always have soy sauce and sweet chili sauce, which are staple ingredients in my kitchen.

1   Preheat the oven to 425°F (or 400°F if using convection).

2   Set the chicken on a sheet pan, baking dish, or cast-iron skillet.

3   Combine the sweet chili sauce, garlic, and sesame seeds in a small bowl.

4   Use a pastry brush to dab the soy sauce all over the chicken. It'll take a couple minutes, and some will fall down into the pan, but try to get as much as possible to absorb into the skin. You can do this step ahead of time if desired, but my grandpa does not.

5   Roast for 30 minutes, then brush the chicken with half the sweet chili mixture.

6   Reduce the oven temperature to 375°F (or 350°F if using convection), roast for 15 minutes, then brush on the rest of the sweet chili mixture and roast for about 15 minutes more, or until a thermometer registers 165°F at the thickest part of the thigh (not touching the bone) or holds at 160°F for 16 seconds. If you cut between the leg and the breast, the skin should be totally opaque and the juices should be clear. Let the chicken rest for about 5 minutes before serving.

7   Depending on the brand of soy sauce you used, the chicken may benefit from a light sprinkle of salt before serving. Definitely taste before adding any!

Za'atar Roast Chicken

GLUTEN-FREE

MAKES 2 TO 4 SERVINGS

1 spatchcocked chicken (you can ask the butcher to do it for you)

Kosher salt to taste

1 shallot, minced

1 date, pitted and chopped

3 garlic cloves, crushed

2 tablespoons extra-virgin olive oil

Freshly ground black pepper to taste

½ cup whole milk Greek yogurt

2 tablespoons za'atar

2 teaspoons ground cumin

½ teaspoon sweet paprika

¼ teaspoon red pepper flakes

1 tablespoon Calabrian chili bomba paste

1 lemon, halved

At a grocery store that has a butcher, you can usually bring any whole chicken you want up to the counter (even the ones in branded third-party packaging) and ask the butcher to spatchcock it for you. While it's not terribly difficult to spatchcock a chicken yourself, I secretly just don't like dealing with the chicken juice. It's all a lot more manageable when they repack it in butcher paper, and they do it for free.

Using a yogurt marinade is one of the tastiest ways to cook chicken. It makes for very moist meat, and you would never know it's yogurt! In this recipe I use za'atar and other Middle Eastern flavors; however, it is possible to take a yogurt marinade in any direction, depending on what spices you add.

1 Set the chicken on a plate and season it generously with salt on all sides; set aside.

2 Mix together the shallot, date, and garlic in a small bowl. Use a pestle, cocktail muddler, or other blunt object to crush them together, then add the olive oil, pepper, yogurt, za'atar, cumin, paprika, red pepper flakes, chili paste, and the juice of ½ lemon (save the other half to squeeze over the finished chicken when serving) and combine well.

3 Brush the mixture all over the chicken. Cover with plastic wrap and marinate in the fridge for at least an hour or preferably overnight.

4 If cooking after about an hour: Put a cast-iron pan in the oven and preheat the oven to 375°F. Place the chicken skin side down on the preheated pan. Roast for 15 minutes before carefully flipping over with tongs. Roast for another 30 to 40 minutes, until the skin is crispy and the internal temperature (in the thickest part of the thigh) reaches 165°F.

5 If marinating overnight: Let the chicken come to room temperature about 30 minutes before cooking. Preheat the oven and the pan while you wait for the chicken to come to room temperature. Cook as written above.

Sausage and Peppers Dinner

DAIRY-FREE
GLUTEN-FREE ... (unless the sausage brand has gluten)

MAKES 2 TO 4 SERVINGS

- 2 tablespoons plus 1 teaspoon neutral oil
- 2 (12-ounce) packages fully cooked chicken sausage, preferably one spicy Italian and one chicken-and-apple sausage, cut into ½-inch slices
- 1 large yellow onion, cut into ½-inch slices
- 2 bell peppers, cut into ½-inch slices
- 2 jalapeños, cut into ¼-inch slices (you can deseed if desired for less heat, but I like the spice)
- ½ teaspoon kosher salt
- ½ teaspoon freshly ground black pepper

This is a classic and easy weekday dinner. I especially like it served over rice. Since it's based on precooked sausages, this recipe eliminates some of the minor inconveniences of cooking with raw meat, and the sausage can live in your fridge a lot longer before you're ready to cook it. It's a good tool to have in your arsenal when you need a quick but filling meal.

1 Heat a large skillet (preferably cast-iron or stainless steel) over medium heat for 1 minute. Add 2 tablespoons of the oil.

2 Add the sausage pieces so that they lay flat on one side. If you can't fit all the sausage in the pan without crowding, start with half and work in batches. Sear until deeply golden brown on one side, 2 to 3 minutes, then flip and cook for an additional 1 to 2 minutes. When the sausage is golden brown, transfer it to a plate and set aside.

3 Add the remaining 1 teaspoon oil to the pan, then add the onions and cook until light brown, 4 to 5 minutes. Add the bell peppers and jalapeños and cook until the peppers start to soften and the onions develop a deeper brown color, 5 to 10 more minutes, then season with the salt and pepper. (Note: the sausage is very seasoned and doesn't need a ton of extra spices.)

4 Stir occasionally to make sure everything gets time in contact with the pan.

5 When you are happy with the texture of the veggies (some people like them really soft, nearly caramelized; others like more firmness), add back in the sausage, toss together, and serve.

Jalapeño Bacon-Wrapped Dates

GLUTEN-FREE
DAIRY-FREE OPTION ... See Smarter Tip below

MAKES 32 DATES (SERVING 6 TO 8)

USE CONVECTION IF YOU HAVE IT

32 small dates (usually pitted are easier to work with)

About 4 ounces cream cheese (see Smarter Tip)

16 slices uncured bacon

2 to 3 jalapeños, sliced in very thin rounds

This is a great hors d'oeuvre (pronounced "horse divorce" in some states) to make if you have friends coming over. My mom used to make traditional bacon-wrapped dates with a little almond inside, and they're delicious that way, but I had the idea to fuse these with a jalapeño popper to create this beautiful monster. Don't use the super-fancy large dates here or the proportion of bacon to dates will be off.

1 Preheat the oven to 400°F (or 375°F if using convection). Line a half sheet pan with aluminum foil. Cut each date open (remove the pit, if needed). Fill each date with roughly ¼ teaspoon cream cheese. Cut the bacon pieces in half crosswise. Wrap each cream cheese–filled date with a half piece of bacon and secure with a toothpick. Arrange on the prepared pan, seam side down. Bake for 15 minutes, until the bacon is crispy, then flip each date over and cook for another 5 minutes, until the bacon fat has mostly rendered. Slide a jalapeño slice over each toothpick and serve.

Smarter Tip

✳ You can substitute an almond for the cream cheese; my mom does. You can also use bleu cheese instead if that is up your alley.

On Fish

The vast majority of recipes in this book are based on dishes that I grew up eating. And while I now enjoy a variety of fish, especially branzino, trout, cod, and tuna, I would be lying if I said these were staple foods in my household growing up. I have a few salmon recipes in the book, because that is mainly what my mom cooked for us at home. Other varieties are things I personally tend to enjoy at restaurants. This is *not* to say that salmon is the only fish suitable for home cooking—in fact, my grandpa Nate often goes to the fishmonger and cooks all sorts of stews and whole fishes. One day, I would love to develop my own take on a wider breadth of fish recipes, but I am still early in that journey.

One tip about fish that may surprise you is that buying it frozen at the grocery store is usually better than "fresh." This may not be the case if you go to a specialty fishmonger, but in general, fish is frozen right after it's caught, so when you buy "fresh" fish at a typical grocery store, it has already been frozen and thawed. Buying it frozen will preserve the freshness, because you can choose to thaw it whenever it's convenient for you.

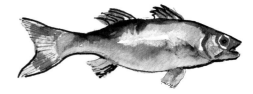

Pomegranate-Glazed Salmon with Coconut Rice

DAIRY-FREE OPTION ... Use oil instead of butter for the rice
GLUTEN-FREE

USE CONVECTION IF YOU HAVE IT

MAKES 2 SERVINGS

For the rice

2 tablespoons butter or neutral oil

2 cups jasmine rice, rinsed well

1 (13.5-ounce) can full-fat coconut milk

1 cup chicken broth or water

2 tablespoons sugar

2 teaspoons kosher salt

1 bunch fresh cilantro, chopped

Lime, for serving

For the fish

2 salmon fillets (about 8 ounces total)

1 cup shishito peppers

2 tablespoons toasted sesame oil

Kosher salt to taste

1 teaspoon potato starch

¼ cup pomegranate molasses

1 shallot, minced

2 bird's eye (Thai) chilies, minced

This recipe is inspired by a dish from a restaurant in New York called Café Gitane. They serve their pomegranate-glazed salmon over a bed of greens with olives and orange supremes. It's a super light and refreshing lunch. This version has a more substantial rice and veggie side, which makes it good for dinner.

1 Preheat the oven to 450°F (or 425°F if using convection).

2 Make the rice: Heat the butter in a medium saucepan over medium heat. When it's hot, add the rinsed rice and toast until some of the rice starts to turn golden brown, 3 to 5 minutes.

3 Add the coconut milk, chicken broth, sugar, and salt.

4 Bring to a boil, then reduce the heat to a simmer over very low heat. Cover the pot, and set a timer for 20 minutes.

5 Make the salmon: Place the salmon in an oven-safe dish and arrange the peppers around it. Drizzle the peppers with the sesame oil and sprinkle with salt, then sprinkle the salmon with salt and a light dusting of potato starch; gently rub it in.

6 Mix together the pomegranate molasses, minced shallot, and chilies in a small bowl; set aside.

7 After the rice is done, turn off the heat, but do NOT open the lid. Let it sit while you cook the salmon. Roast the salmon for 12 to 15 minutes. After the first 5 minutes of cooking, spoon half the pomegranate molasses mixture over the salmon; repeat with the remaining pomegranate molasses mixture 2 minutes later. When the salmon is ready, you'll start to see a bit of white coming out between the striations, and it should become more opaque. Salmon is okay to eat medium.

8 Once the salmon is done, the rice should also be done steaming. Remove the lid, fluff it up with a fork, and mix in the cilantro and a squeeze of lime juice. Serve the salmon with the peppers and rice.

MORE EASY SALMON RECIPES ON THE FOLLOWING PAGES.

Sweet Chili Miso Salmon

MAKES 2 SERVINGS

DAIRY-FREE
GLUTEN-FREE OPTION ... Use tamari or gluten-free soy sauce and gluten-free miso for the marinade

2 salmon fillets (about 8 ounces total)

Sweet Chili Miso Marinade (page 126)

Since fish is more delicate than chicken or red meat, I find this cooking method easiest because it doesn't require any flipping or risk it all falling apart. That said, you can use whatever method you prefer; my mom, for example, is partial to grilling.

1 Put the salmon in a bowl or a ziplock bag. Pour the marinade over it and make sure the salmon is evenly coated in the sauce. Cover the bowl or seal the bag and refrigerate for 1 to 2 hours before cooking.

2 Preheat your broiler to 500°F. Transfer the salmon to an oven-safe baking dish, letting the excess marinade drip back into the bowl or bag, but without patting it dry. Discard the leftover marinade.

3 Broil for 11 to 13 minutes, depending on desired doneness. (When the salmon is ready, you'll start to see a bit of white coming out between the striations, and it should become more opaque.)

Sheet Pan Teriyaki Salmon and Veggies

MAKES 4 SERVINGS

DAIRY-FREE
GLUTEN-FREE OPTION ... Use tamari or gluten-free soy sauce

USE CONVECTION IF YOU HAVE IT

⅓ cup soy sauce or tamari

⅓ cup unseasoned rice wine vinegar

2 tablespoons sugar

½ teaspoon red pepper flakes

½ teaspoon garlic powder

4 salmon fillets (1 pound total)

1 head broccoli, cut in small florets

½ teaspoon kosher salt

2 tablespoons neutral oil

I love a meal where the sides and proteins are cooked at the same time. As opposed to the miso-marinated salmon recipe on page 167, which is cooked under the broiler, I use a slightly lower temperature here to allow the broccoli enough time to cook without burning.

1 Preheat the oven to 450°F (or 425°F if using convection) and line a half sheet pan with aluminum foil.

2 Combine the soy sauce, rice wine vinegar, and sugar in a small saucepan. Bring the mixture to a boil, then reduce the heat to medium-low and simmer for 1 minute. Remove from the heat and stir in the red pepper flakes and garlic powder.

3 Put the salmon on the prepared baking sheet. Arrange the broccoli florets around the salmon. Sprinkle the broccoli with the salt and drizzle with the oil. Pour the sauce over the salmon (it's okay if it migrates to the broccoli). Cook for about 20 minutes, or until the salmon reaches your desired doneness. (When the salmon is ready, you'll start to see a bit of white coming out between the striations, and it should become more opaque.)

Repurposing Leftover Salmon

My family was influenced by food personality Emily Mariko to make leftover salmon into delicious salmon rice bowls. We have found that this can work when there is just a bit left over for a serving of one or in larger quantities. Sometimes when entertaining larger groups, we like to make a whole side of grilled salmon which can be served at room temperature with rice and lots of toppings. In our extended family, we have people with various dietary preferences, so this dinner allows everyone to personalize their own bowls. We like to offer toppings such as edamame, cabbage slaw, mango, marinated cucumbers, chopped cilantro, scallions, Japanese mayo, sriracha, soy sauce, and toasted sesame seeds, but you can get creative.

Oven Crispy Tofu

MAKES 3 OR 4 SERVINGS

For the Tofu

1 (14- to 16-ounce) block extra-firm tofu

2 tablespoons neutral oil

2 tablespoons potato starch

Suggested seasonings

1 teaspoon garlic powder

1 teaspoon kosher salt

½ teaspoon freshly ground black pepper

¼ teaspoon red pepper flakes

Sweet chili sauce (optional), for serving

I like breaking up the tofu with my hands to get a rough surface—more area to get crispy! This method is a great way to make tofu and you can switch up the sauce and seasonings to adapt it to other cuisines.

1 Preheat the oven to 400°F (or 375°F if using convection).

2 Press your tofu: sandwich it between two paper towels, set it on a plate, and set another plate on top and weight it with a heavy book. Let sit for about 10 minutes (you don't need to dry it out more than that).

3 Crumble the tofu in irregular pieces (roughly 1-inch cubes) into a bowl. Mix in the oil, potato starch, and any desired seasonings, then spread out the tofu on a large baking sheet.

4 Bake for about 20 minutes, or until crispy. If desired, turn off the oven and leave the tofu in for an additional 10 minutes (for extra crispiness!).

5 The tofu is great as is or tossed in sweet chili sauce.

Oven Crispy Tofu (page 172) with
Easy Green Beans (page 64)

Sweets

. . . what I'm really here for

"I'm a Cook, Not a Baker"

Friends, family, and viewers often tell me that they cook but "can't bake." While it is true that baking is a more exact science than cooking, I've never seen the skills as inherently different.

To make the baking recipes in this book as approachable as possible, I chose to include only recipes that could be made without an electric mixer or specialty equipment. If you have a half sheet pan (which you need for many of the savory recipes in this book), an 8 × 8-inch baking dish (which is also very versatile), and a muffin tin, you will be able to whip up all these recipes. If you do have an electric mixer, by all means use it, but you can make all of these recipes with a good spatula, wooden spoon, and a whisk.

While you can't mess around as much with the ratios, there are still ways to make baking recipes your own. If you are tempted to change up the flavor, consider first whether an ingredient is there for structure or flavor. Ingredients such as eggs, flour, butter, and sugar do add flavor, but they also tend to be the structural foundation of a baked good. I do not recommend adjusting these ingredients unless you *really* know what you're doing. On the other hand, there are many ingredients that you can change up to create drastically different flavor combinations. For example, citrus zest contains much of the flavor of the fruit and can really elevate the flavor of a pastry or cake; unlike the juice, it won't affect the overall ratios of the batter. Ground spices are also a good thing to play around with, whether it be cinnamon, ginger, cardamom, or even sumac.

Vanilla Sugar

VEGAN
VEGETARIAN
DAIRY-FREE
GLUTEN-FREE

Granulated sugar, any amount up to 5 pounds (it's best to store it in a large resealable container)

1 vanilla bean (see Smarter Tip)

This luxurious flavored sugar may seem complex, but it is actually one of the easiest things to make. With minimal effort, you will have amazing vanilla-scented sugar that boosts flavor in any recipe. It is especially good in custards, vanilla cakes, shortbread, or anything where vanilla is the principal flavor. If you like your coffee sweet, try using this to make the best vanilla latte.

1   Stick a vanilla bean in your sugar. You can even use one from which you've already stripped the seeds for something else. Using an already-used bean will give you the most bang for your buck. Just make sure to pat it dry before using if you steeped it in a liquid.

2   Close the container and let sit for at least 24 hours. The flavor will get stronger over time, but you can start using it after 24 hours.

3   Use like regular sugar—it's best in recipes where vanilla is the main flavor.

Smarter Tip

* Vanilla beans can be quite expensive, especially at the grocery store. For this reason, I strongly recommend buying your vanilla in a higher quantity online. I buy my vanilla beans online from Vanilla Products USA.

Homemade Vanilla Extract

VEGAN
VEGETARIAN
DAIRY-FREE
GLUTEN-FREE

6 vanilla beans (see Smarter Tip, page 177)

8 ounces (235ml) cheap vodka, rum, or tequila

Smarter Tips

* You could use light rum or tequila instead of vodka. If you can't use alcohol for personal or religious reasons, you could substitute food-grade glycerin.

* Infinite vanilla hack: after the extract gets really strong from several months of sitting, you can periodically top it off with more vodka and occasionally add another vanilla pod or two. Go by color so you don't dilute it too much. Once in a blue moon, you can take out all the vanilla pods and replace them with fresh ones, but vanilla does not spoil, so you can make this last for years and you don't need to fuss over it too much.

Let's get this straight: "Bourbon vanilla" does not mean vanilla extract made with bourbon. Bourbon actually refers to a type of vanilla named after a French-colonized island now called Reunion Island. Other than both alluding to French influence, the alcohol bourbon and the Bourbon islands are not related.

Inevitably, whenever I explain this, I always get a comment saying, "Well, my family DOES use bourbon and it's the best!" Here's the thing: flavoring your nice bourbon with vanilla is not the end of the world—to quote Ina Garten, "How bad could that be?"—but that doesn't mean it's smart to use bourbon in vanilla extract.

Vanilla is one of the most expensive and complex spices, with more than 250 flavor compounds inside. To fully appreciate the flavor, you should use a flavorless alcohol such as vodka or Everclear. That means you start with a blank slate and get the full spectrum of flavors. If you make your vanilla extract in bourbon, it masks the flavor of the vanilla and you're stuck adding bourbon to everything you want vanilla in. **My advice: make it in a flavorless alcohol, and if you still want to add the flavor of bourbon into a baked good, you can add it separately!**

Homemade vanilla extract has just two ingredients—neutral alcohol and vanilla pods—unlike many commercial extracts that contain dyes, sugars, and other additives. You also get the benefit of the little vanilla seeds in your extract, which amplify flavor and give a luxurious appearance in baked goods. Plus it's cheaper! Your homemade extract will last indefinitely and you'll never again buy it at the store.

Deeper Dive

* **Price comparison** (at the time of writing):
  $6 Tito's vodka (8 ounces) + $15 of vanilla beans = $2.60/ounce
  Nielsen-Massey (leading brand) vanilla extract = $4.32/ounce
  And that's before infinitely topping it off once it's strong. (You can also use a cheaper alcohol than Tito's.)

1 Using a sharp knife, split the vanilla beans lengthwise. Stick them in a glass bottle. Fill the bottle with the vodka and close it.

2 Shake once or twice daily for 4 weeks (optional). After 8 weeks, use as normal vanilla extract. It'll get better the longer it sits.

VANILLA EXTRACT
5/7/2022

Vanilla Cream Cheese Frosting

1 (8-ounce/226g) package full-fat cream cheese (such as Philadelphia), at room temperature

8 tablespoons (1 stick/113g) unsalted butter, at room temperature

1 (1-pound/454g) box powdered sugar

About 1 teaspoon vanilla extract

Cream cheese frosting is my favorite. Classically it pairs with red velvet and carrot cake, but I also love its tangy flavor on any chocolate or vanilla cake.

A small but vocal minority of people claim they HATE cream cheese frosting. It is my theory that most of these people get hung up on the words "cream cheese" and start imagining everything bagels, but if you just told them it was "vanilla frosting," they'd think it was the tastiest one they've ever had!

Start with really room-temperature butter and cream cheese (the softer it is, the easier it will be to mix), and then if you need to, pop the finished icing in the refrigerator to firm up a little. Here are the amounts I find most useful—enough to frost a batch of cupcakes or a layer cake—but feel free to scale the recipe up or down depending on what you're making.

1   Beat the cream cheese and butter by hand (or with an electric hand mixer, if you have one) until well combined and creamy.

2   Add half the powdered sugar, beating until very well combined, then add the remaining powdered sugar and beat again until very well combined.

3   Beat in the vanilla extract.

4   Use right away, or if it seems too soft, you may want to refrigerate the icing for a few minutes before using to firm up.

Favorite Vanilla Cake or Cupcakes

VEGETARIAN

MAKES ABOUT 18 CUPCAKES, TWO 8 X 8-INCH CAKE LAYERS,
OR TWO 8-INCH ROUNDS

1⅓ cups (175g) cake flour (not self-rising)

1 cup (200g) sugar (or Vanilla Sugar, page 177)

1½ teaspoons baking powder

½ teaspoon baking soda

½ teaspoon kosher salt

4 tablespoons (½ stick/57g) unsalted butter, at room temperature

¼ cup (60ml) neutral oil

2 large eggs

⅓ cup (75g) whole milk Greek yogurt

1 tablespoon vanilla extract (homemade, page 178, or store-bought) or paste

⅔ cup (160ml) whole milk

Vanilla Cream Cheese Frosting (page 180)

This is *the* cake recipe for people who claim they don't like cake. It's light, moist, and not too sweet. I've been making this for years, and people consistently tell me that it is the best vanilla cake they've ever had.

The only ingredient in this recipe that I don't necessarily consider to be a "staple" is cake flour. While I do believe that cake flour is worth buying for this recipe, you can also make a quick substitute, using all-purpose flour but substituting 2 tablespoons of it with potato starch. This mimics cake flour's lower protein content, which makes the cupcakes lighter and airier.

This recipe is based on one from the blog *Cupcake Project* but has been simplified and adapted over the many years I've been using it.

1   Preheat the oven to 350°F. Line muffin tins with cupcake liners or grease enough wells for 18 to 20 cupcakes, or butter and flour two 8-inch square or 8-inch round cake pans. To be sure my cakes release easily from the tins, I line the bottom with parchment paper. For best results, grease the pans, add the parchment, grease again, then flour.

2   Mix the flour, sugar, baking powder, baking soda, and salt in a large bowl.

3   Add the butter and mix until it is well dispersed in the flour mixture. This can be done with a mixer, but I usually use my hands and rub the butter into the dry ingredients until there are no chunks, just tiny crumbs similar to the texture of sand.

4   Add the oil, eggs, yogurt, and vanilla. Beat until incorporated.

5   Pour in the milk and mix until smooth. The batter should be quite thin.

6   Fill cupcake liners half to two-thirds of the way up, or divide the batter between the prepared pans.

7   Bake until the cupcakes or cakes spring back when lightly pressed, 14 to 20 minutes for cupcakes, or 25 to 30 minutes for

RECIPE CONTINUES

cakes. Keep in mind that each oven is different and the cake pans you choose can affect the baking time.

8 Let cool in the pans for 15 minutes, and then take the cupcakes or cakes out and let cool completely on a wire rack before icing. You may need to run a knife around the edges of the pans to help release the cake.

9 Frost the cake with the Vanilla Cream Cheese Frosting (see my Cake Decorating Tips on page 186).

Deeper Dive: What makes this recipe so good?

✳ The "reverse creaming" method (mixing softened butter into the flour mixture, rather than adding the flour after creaming) gives the cake a fine crumb.

✳ The cake uses half oil (for moistness) and half butter (for flavor and crumb structure).

✳ The Greek yogurt tenderizes and moistens the cake.

✳ The cake flour (I use Swans Down or King Arthur) gives it a lighter texture.

Cake Decorating Tips

This book focuses on one-bowl, easy-to-make desserts. My Favorite Vanilla Cake (page 183) can be made into layer cakes, but it's a lot less work to make into a single layer sheet cake as pictured. **These tips are for those of you interested in taking your cake decorating to the next level.**

1. **Make cake decorating a two-day process.** If you are making a layer cake with frosting on all sides, this is my #1 tip. After baking and cooling your cake layers, wrap them in plastic wrap and freeze them overnight, or until you want to decorate the cakes. You can keep them well wrapped in the freezer for at least two weeks! Freezing cake layers not only helps to keep your cakes moist, but cold cakes are also *much easier* to handle and decorate. In addition, it's much less labor-intensive to spread the work and cleanup across two days.

2. **Invest in the right tools.** In this book, everything can be made with limited equipment. But if you find yourself making a lot of cakes, it may be worth investing in a few extra tools. If your cake layers come out of the oven very domed, a serrated bread knife is great for leveling the tops. Leveling cakes ensures that they stack neatly and don't have weird indentations in between the layers. The other tools I always use when I'm decorating a cake are a small offset spatula, medium offset spatula, metal bench/cake scraper, cardboard cake round, and a rotating cake stand. The offset spatulas are great for spreading frosting without your arm getting in the way. Cardboard cake boards make cakes really easy to transport, and they are completely flat, unlike most plates, which make it really hard to smooth around the bottom evenly. I buy them for less than a dollar each at my local baking supply store. I usually get a board 2 to 3 inches wider in diameter than my cake pans.

3. **Use a frosting with a light consistency.** A fluffy frosting will be much easier to spread than a thick one. You want it thin enough to spread nicely but thick enough to hold its shape when it's on the cake. In this book, I chose to include only dessert recipes that do not require an electric mixer. My Vanilla Cream Cheese Frosting (page 180) can be done totally by hand, and it's my personal favorite. If you do have a mixer, you can check out my website, scheckeats.com, for my full guide on buttercreams, which really cannot be done by hand.

4. **Decide if you want a crumb coat.** Have you ever iced a cake only to find your frosting littered with crumbs? I used to assume that good cake decorators possessed secret cake-whispering powers because somehow their

cakes never got crumbs in the frosting. As it turns out, they were just doing a crumb coat! All it involves is covering the cake in the thinnest-possible layer of frosting and then refrigerating it before putting on the final coat. It takes only around 15 to 20 minutes to solidify in the fridge, and it works like a primer to lock in all the crumbs. When you frost the cake on top of that, nothing gets mixed in. If you don't have extra time for this, you can work around it if you use a lot of buttercream and your cakes are frozen thoroughly.

5. **Don't stress.** Nobody expects your cake to look like it came out of Magnolia Bakery. Relax! It's supposed to be fun. Say it with me: "This is fun, I am having fun." It can be hard to decide when to stop putting on finishing touches. At a certain point, you'll be doing more harm than good—stop before you get there!

✳ That's sixteen-year-old me teaching cake decorating at Williams-Sonoma.

Brown Butter Chocolate Chip Cookies

VEGETARIAN

ALL STAPLE INGREDIENTS

MAKES ABOUT 42 COOKIES

1 cup (2 sticks/226g) unsalted butter

1½ cups (300g) firmly packed dark brown sugar (Trader Joe's brand is fine, too, but don't use light)

¼ cup (50g) granulated sugar

2¼ cups (315g) all-purpose flour (see Smarter Tips)

1 teaspoon baking soda

½ teaspoon kosher salt, plus flaky salt for sprinkling (can use more kosher salt)

1 large egg plus 1 egg yolk

2 teaspoons vanilla extract

1 tablespoon whole milk Greek yogurt

1 (12-ounce) bag chocolate chips (about 2 cups; I like semisweet or a mixture of bittersweet and milk chocolate)

Brown butter is all the rage now, and, not to be that guy, but my friends were making these cookies way before it was cool. To me, chocolate chip cookies are such a staple, you should have more than one recipe in your arsenal: a quick version you can whip up in a second (see mine on page 192) and a gourmet version.

Nearly a decade ago, my friend Kaela had been keeping this gem of a recipe among her closest family and friends. If you were very lucky, Kaela might have made them for your birthday. They are her family's *specialty*.

On one fateful day, she gave the recipe to our mutual friend, Maia. Maia was allowed to make them with me, but she was on strict orders to "NOT GIVE THE RECIPE TO JEREMY."

Well, after I made them with Maia and realized that the perfect cookie was not even that hard to make, I had no choice but to find the recipe. Fortunately, after a little online sleuthing, I found the cookies hailed from a food blog called *Ambitious Kitchen*.

After way more high school drama than was really necessary, my friends agreed that it would be fine if I made the cookies. Kaela, Maia, and I still closely protected the recipe because it is THAT good! I am thrilled to share it with you now.

1 Place the butter in a medium skillet over low heat.

2 While the butter begins to melt, combine the brown sugar and granulated sugar in a large bowl.

3 After the butter melts, raise the heat to medium and continue cooking, mixing gently with a spoon or whisk. The butter will foam, then the foam will subside. After a few minutes, the butter will develop a nutty, toffee-like aroma. At this point, it is almost ready. Lower the heat to medium-low and cook until the milk solids turn golden brown.

4 Pour the hot butter over the sugar mixture and whisk to combine. Set aside to cool for 5 minutes.

5 Meanwhile, whisk the flour, baking soda, and kosher salt in a small bowl. In another small bowl, whisk together the egg, egg yolk, vanilla, and yogurt.

6 Pour the egg mixture into the cooled brown butter–sugar mixture in small additions, whisking to combine. Whisk until most of the sugar granules dissolve.

7 Add the flour mixture and mix gently to combine.

8 Reserve about ⅔ cup of the chocolate chips to add on top of the individual cookie balls. This will make them more "picture perfect." Fold the rest of the chocolate chips into the dough.

9 Refrigerate the dough for 2 hours, then scoop the dough into small balls (about 1½ tablespoons) onto a cookie sheet lined with parchment paper or a silicone baking mat (such as Silpat). Or, for faster chilling, freeze the dough for 5 minutes, then scoop it into balls and freeze the balls for 30 minutes.

10 About half an hour before you're ready to bake, preheat the oven to 350°F.

11 Before baking, sprinkle each ball of dough with flaky salt and top with 3 or 4 reserved chocolate chips.

12 Bake for about 10 minutes, until puffed and lightly browned around the edges. The cookies should not be set in the center. For best results, bake one sheet at a time.

13 Let cool on the pan for 10 minutes, then transfer to a wire rack to cool completely.

SEE PHOTO ON NEXT SPREAD

Smarter Tips

✳ I keep the scooped dough ready to go in my freezer at all times for emergencies. You can bake directly from frozen on an as-needed basis—just add 1 to 2 minutes to the baking time. Great for when you have surprise company over or just need one singular cookie on a bad day—I use my toaster oven!

✳ If making these without a scale: Even though the correct way to measure flour by volume is to fluff it up with a spoon and then spoon the flour into the measuring cup before leveling it off, for this recipe, just scoop the measuring cup directly into the bag of flour and level. You'll end up with a more tightly packed cup that better corresponds to the correct weight.

✳ The cookies can be stored for a few days in an airtight container. To help them retain their chewiness, store the cookies with a slice of bread.

Bakery-Style Chocolate Chip Cookies

MAKES 18 COOKIES

1 cup (2 sticks/226g) unsalted butter, at room temperature

½ cup (100g) granulated sugar

1½ cups (300g) packed dark brown sugar

2 large eggs

2 teaspoons vanilla extract

3 cups (390g) all-purpose flour

2 teaspoons hot water

1 teaspoon baking soda

½ teaspoon kosher salt, plus flaky sea salt for sprinkling (can use more kosher salt)

1 (12-ounce) bag semisweet chocolate chips

Smarter Tip

✳ For smaller cookies, use a 1½ tablespoon scoop; bake for 10 to 14 minutes. This will make about 40 cookies.

This recipe does not require chilling, making it perfect for when you need your cookie fix right away. True to bakery style, these are much larger than the brown butter version! Compare them to the brown butter recipe on page 188 and see which you prefer!

1 Preheat the oven to 375°F. Line two half sheet pans with parchment paper or silicone baking mats (such as Silpat).

2 If you have a mixer you can use it here, or use a wooden spoon or Danish dough whisk to cream the butter with the sugars in a large bowl until well combined, about 2 minutes. Don't rush it.

3 Add the eggs one at time, and beat for a full minute after each incorporation. Scrape the bowl down as necessary. Beat in the vanilla.

4 Slowly mix in the flour.

5 Pour the hot water over the baking soda in a small cup or tiny bowl and stir to dissolve. Add the baking soda to the dough and mix thoroughly.

6 Mix in the kosher salt and chocolate chips.

7 You'll bake the cookies one tray at a time, so do this with the first baking sheet and repeat with the succeeding batches:

8 Use an ice cream scoop (about ¼ cup) to scoop six large mounds of dough onto a prepared pan (leaving plenty of room to let them spread). Sprinkle a little flaky salt on each mound.

9 Bake for 12 to 16 minutes, until the cookies are browned around the edges and not quite set in the middle.

10 Let cool on the pan for 5 to 10 minutes, until firm enough to remove with a metal spatula, then transfer to a wire rack to cool completely, or eat them warm. As the first batch cooks, prepare the next one. By the time you're ready to bake the third batch, the first pan should be cool enough to reuse. Enjoy!

The Case Against Bottled Citrus

When I call for citrus, it has to be fresh. Let me be clear, I do not share this to create undeserved fear of engineered food products. I don't think that food products are "bad" just because they are engineered. Food science and engineering are critical to ensure food safety, quality, and accessibility. But in this case, I believe bottled pasteurized citrus juice tastes much worse than the fresh stuff, and it's not that hard to squeeze it yourself. One hack to easily get more juice out of your citrus is to squeeze it between the arms of your tongs. I also do like citrus pressing tools since I use citrus juices a lot, but I wouldn't characterize those tools as a necessity.

Did you know bottled citrus juice that is ostensibly 100 percent juice can actually be completely flavored with engineered chemicals?[16] When this juice is processed, manufacturers remove the oxygen to increase the shelf life up to a year. Unfortunately, taking out the oxygen also completely gets rid of other naturally occurring chemicals responsible for the fresh taste. As Alissa Hamilton, PhD, JD, reports, companies like Tropicana add back in "flavor packs," produced by the same companies that make Dior fragrances. Since they engineer the flavorings from orange essence and oil, juice companies are not obligated to disclose them as added ingredients. Technically this is still considered "natural flavor," since it's derived from fruit, but as Hamilton notes, "the flavor packs . . . resemble nothing found in nature."

To be clear, it's an immediate red flag when people warn you about "chemicals" in food without adding any nuance. Everything is chemicals! Water is a chemical! You are made of chemicals. The problem is not that these foods contain *added* chemicals, or that they're engineered; it's that it feels misleading when they are labeled 100 percent juice.

If you enjoy them, or if the convenience outweighs the difference in quality for you, that's your prerogative. However, it is important to know that pasteurized citrus products are really extremely far off in flavor from the fresh versions. If you must use bottled, cold-pressed citrus juices are superior in flavor to pasteurized. Cold-pressing uses high pressure and refrigeration instead of pasteurization to prevent bacterial growth.[17] The downside is that these juices tend to be very expensive, so I still think the best option is squeezing the fruit yourself.

Whipped Cream

MAKES ABOUT 2 CUPS

VEGETARIAN
GLUTEN-FREE

ALL STAPLE INGREDIENTS

1 cup heavy cream

1 to 3 tablespoons powdered sugar, granulated sugar, caster sugar, or vanilla sugar (to taste)

½ teaspoon vanilla extract

Smarter Tip

✳ You can use other flavorings instead of vanilla. I love strawberry puree, ground cinnamon, or cocoa powder.

Unlike whipped cream, Cool Whip is mostly water, hydrogenated oils, and high-fructose corn syrup. I'm not going to lie, sometimes it hits the spot the way frosting in a can does, but it's in a league of its own . . . It's not whipped cream.

Depending on the brand, the cream ideal for whipping can be labeled as "heavy whipping cream" or "heavy cream," or "double cream" in some countries, and has a butterfat content of 35 to 40 percent. I look for no additional ingredients and prefer varieties that are not "ultrapasteurized"—a local brand or dairy is probably your best bet for this.

You can whip the cream by hand with your biggest balloon whisk, electric hand beaters, or a stand mixer. No matter which you are using, place your whisk, metal beaters, or whisk attachment in the freezer with your metal bowl 5 minutes prior to whipping. The colder everything is, the faster and better your cream will whip.

After everything is well chilled, remove the bowl and whisk from your freezer and the cream from your refrigerator and pour your cream, sugar, and vanilla into your chilled bowl. Don't worry about being too exact with the sugar—you can always add more. Reserve a few tablespoons of cream in case you overwhip it.

1 Whisk or beat your cream, starting slowly and gradually increasing your speed. If you are whisking by hand, the best way to do this is with a fast, side-to-side motion.

2 Beat until the cream is noticeably thicker and reaches soft peaks, 2 to 4 minutes. This means that when you remove your whisk from the cream, any "peaks" of cream clinging to the whisk quickly soften. If you plan on piping your whipped cream, you will want it to reach medium or stiff peaks by beating slightly longer. Do this at a lower speed, as your cream will quickly reach medium and stiff peaks. If your cream becomes grainy, you have overwhipped it. To fix it, add a few tablespoons of unwhipped cream into the whipped cream and mix it back to the consistency you want.

Tangy Key Lime Pie with Gingersnap Crust

VEGETARIAN
GLUTEN-FREE OPTION ... If you can find gluten-free gingersnaps or graham crackers for the crust

MAKES ONE 9-INCH PIE

8 to 9 ounces (250g) ginger cookies or Biscoff cookies

6 tablespoons (90g) unsalted butter, melted

Pinch of kosher salt

2 (14-ounce) cans sweetened condensed milk

Finely grated zest from 4 limes

1 cup (240 ml) FRESH lime juice (from 2 to 3 pounds limes; you can use regular or key limes)

4 egg yolks

Whipped Cream (page 195), for topping

Smarter Tip

✳ While I usually consider limes a staple ingredient, in this recipe they are more of a star, since you'll need a lot of them to yield enough juice for the pie.

This is one of the lowest-effort, highest-reward desserts, and honestly my personal favorite. It is the recipe I make for my own birthday!

If you don't have a deep-dish pie plate, this recipe can be made in an 8 × 8-inch square baking dish; it'll be more like key lime pie bars, and equally as good.

"Regular" limes, technically Persian limes, are much larger than key limes. If you happen to see fresh key limes at the store, they are worth getting. That said, they can be a pain to squeeze because they're so small. Many stores also sell bottled key lime juice. I suggest *never* using the bottled stuff, even if the Florida purists say it's more "authentic." I would much rather have pie made from fresh Persian limes than bottled key lime juice (see The Case Against Bottled Citrus, page 194).

1 Preheat the oven to 350°F.

2 Crush the cookies in a blender or food processor or in a gallon-size freezer bag using a rolling pin or a wine bottle (gently). When they are crushed to fine crumbs, add the butter and salt to the blender or bag and shake or process to combine.

3 Press the crumbs into a 9-inch deep-dish pie plate, using the bottom of a measuring cup to pack them tightly.

4 Bake for 15 minutes, until the crust is lightly toasted. Set aside.

5 Whisk together the sweetened condensed milk, lime zest, lime juice, and egg yolks in a large (at least 4-cup capacity) measuring cup or medium bowl until completely combined.

6 Gently pour the filling into the baked crust and return to the oven, still at 350°F, for 15 to 20 minutes, until the filling is mostly set, but the center quivers slightly when gently shaken. Let cool to room temperature.

7 Loosely cover with aluminum foil and refrigerate at least 8 hours (overnight is better).

8 When the pie is completely chilled, top to taste with freshly whipped cream.

Pretzel Blondies

MAKES 15 TO 20 BLONDIES
(DEPENDING ON HOW YOU CUT THEM)

1½ cups (195g) all-purpose flour

1 teaspoon baking powder

Pinch of kosher salt

12 tablespoons (1½ sticks/170g)
   unsalted butter, melted

1½ cups (300g) packed dark
   brown sugar

2 large eggs

4 teaspoons vanilla extract
   (yes, it's a lot!)

Chocolate chips to taste
   (1 to 2 cups)

Lightly crushed pretzels to taste
   (about 1 cup)

Flaky sea salt (or you can use
   more kosher salt), for garnish

Blondies are what I make whenever I have to bring dessert to an event but really don't have the time or energy to overthink it. Because blondies are pretty much a blank canvas, it takes very little effort to make them special with a few fun mix-ins, and they are a total crowd-pleaser. With no mixer or chilling required, these take less than half an hour from start to finish.

1   Preheat the oven to 350°F. Line a 9 × 13-inch baking pan with aluminum foil or parchment paper, leaving an inch of overhang for easy release, and butter the edges or spray with baking spray.

2   Whisk together the flour, baking powder, and salt in a small bowl.

3   Whisk the butter and brown sugar together in a large bowl until well combined. Add the eggs one at a time and whisk very well. Mix in the vanilla extract.

4   Dump the dry ingredients over the wet and use a rubber spatula to fold them in. Fold in the chocolate chips and pretzels.

5   Spread the batter into the prepared pan and sprinkle with flaky salt. Bake for 22 to 25 minutes, until lightly golden brown and dry on top. Let cool for at least 30 minutes before lifting out onto a cutting board and cutting into squares.

Favorite Banana Bread

VEGETARIAN

MAKES 1 LOAF

3 ripe bananas (very, very ripe)

5½ tablespoons (⅓ cup/75g) melted unsalted butter

1 teaspoon baking soda

Pinch of kosher salt

½ to 1 cup (100 to 200g) granulated sugar (I usually use right around ¾ cup, but I adjust according to the ripeness of my bananas)

1 large egg

1 teaspoon vanilla extract

1½ cups (195g) all-purpose flour

1 teaspoon ground cinnamon

1 tablespoon raw, turbinado, or demerara sugar, for sprinkling (or use more granulated sugar)

As much as my mom tries to instill it in me, I am not usually a "less is more" kind of person. In life, that applies to the number of shoes in (or rather spilling out of) my closet, and in baking it often refers to all the embellishments I might try to use in a recipe. In so many recipes, for example, browning the butter instead of simply melting it adds a delightful depth of flavor. I also love adding Greek yogurt or sour cream to baked goods, which adds moisture, fluff, and richness. I might sub in brown sugar for white, hoping the molasses flavor will add that extra something . . . but not here. This really is a less-is-more kind of recipe.

While I grew up calling this recipe "Dr. Hogewood's Banana Bread," as it was the one a friend's dad would make, I later learned it originated from Elise Bauer's *Simply Recipes* website. Other than adapting the recipe to my communication style, the only thing I really do differently is add cinnamon, and sometimes chocolate chips if I am feeling extra frisky. There are a lot of banana bread recipes out there that need a stand mixer and a million extra ingredients, and I've tried dozens . . . and I always come back to this easy one.

My youngest brother, Evan, has always loved this banana bread especially if I make it plain, without any add-ins. He even requested it instead of birthday cake at his parties when he was little. I've also adapted it into a muffin version (page 203). It's almost the same, but the leavening and cook times are a bit different.

1 Preheat the oven to 350°F. Grease an 8 × 4-inch loaf pan.

2 Mash the bananas with a fork in a medium bowl.

3 Whisking briefly between each addition, add the butter, baking soda, salt, sugar, egg, vanilla, flour, and cinnamon.

4 Pour the batter into the prepared pan and sprinkle the top with the raw sugar.

5 Bake for 50 to 60 minutes (erring on the side of less) until golden brown and cooked through; the edges of the cake will start to pull away from the pan.

6 Let cool in the pan for 10 to 15 minutes, then turn out onto a wire rack to cool completely. Slice with a bread knife.

TURN THE PAGE FOR THE MUFFIN VARIATION

Banana Muffins

To make banana muffins, grease a standard 12-well muffin tin or line it with muffin liners. Add ¼ teaspoon baking powder to the batter after you add the baking soda. You could also add 1⅓ cups chocolate chips (or more or less, whatever your preference), if desired. Use a large ice cream scoop to fill each well of the prepared pan about two-thirds of the way up. When you scrape out every last bit of batter, you'll have just enough for 12 muffins. Sprinkle the tops of each with raw sugar or extra chocolate chips. Bake for 16 to 18 minutes, until the muffins are puffed tall and spring back when lightly pressed on top. Let the muffins cool for 5 minutes in the pan before using an offset spatula or a paring knife to loosen the sides and remove the muffins. Enjoy warm, or set on a wire rack to cool completely.

Cranberry Carrot Cake

MAKES ONE 8 X 8-INCH CAKE

4 tablespoons (57g) unsalted butter, melted

¼ cup (54 grams) neutral oil

1 cup (200g) packed dark brown sugar

2 large eggs

1¼ cups grated carrots (approximately 6 medium carrots), squeezed in a towel to remove excess liquid

1 cup (100g) dried cranberries

1 cup (130g) all-purpose flour

½ teaspoon baking soda

1 teaspoon baking powder

2 teaspoons ground cinnamon

½ teaspoon kosher salt

1-inch piece fresh ginger, grated

¼ cup (70g) whole milk Greek yogurt

This is a very simple mini sheet cake that I make in an 8 × 8-inch baking pan. You can serve it unfrosted as a "snacking cake" or add Vanilla Cream Cheese Frosting on top (page 180). You will only need about half of the frosting from that recipe.

1 Preheat the oven to 375°F (or 350°F if using convection). Line an 8 × 8-inch baking pan with aluminum foil or parchment paper, leaving 1 inch of overhang (to easily lift out the cake when done), and spray with baking spray.

2 Whisk together the butter, oil, brown sugar, and eggs in a large bowl.

3 Stir in the carrots and cranberries.

4 Add in the flour, baking soda, baking powder, cinnamon, salt, and fresh ginger; mix just until the flour is incorporated.

5 Add the yogurt and mix just until blended.

6 Bake for about 30 minutes, until the cake springs back when you press it lightly in the center. Let cool completely before lifting the cake from the pan and serving.

Acknowledgments

It feels daunting to thank everyone who has made a positive impact on this book. That's a miracle in and of itself—to know there were hundreds, thousands, and even millions of people encouraging me along the way. While it would be impossible to name each individual, I am so thankful for every single one of my viewers, readers, and everybody who has supported me throughout the years.

Mom, I know you prefer to wing it in the kitchen instead of following the details of a written recipe, but you played an integral role in this book. A big part of it comes directly from your kitchen and the wisdom you passed along to me. Thank you for contributing your recipes, testing mine, and always being available to give a second opinion on anything I write. I'm glad that so many of our family recipes are compiled in one place now, so we'll have an accurate record and be able to re-create the best ones easily.

Dad, thank you for passing on to me your love of food. You and I are the type of people who are already planning our next meal while we are still eating the current one . . . and I think that's special. I also get my ability to sense distinct tastes on the palate from you, and I love that we share that. Even though I often kick you out of the kitchen, I always appreciate your honest reviews of my food.

To my brothers Leo, Gabriel, and Evan, please lower your voices; I am trying to concentrate.

To Grandma Karen, thank you for sharing your love of cookbooks and cooking with me. You are our family's original recipe developer. I can always count on you to find the most important details in a recipe and provide meticulous feedback. Thank you for sharing your iconic recipes. I'll make them for us all so you can lie down and put your feet up.

To Grandma Nan, thank you for lending your artistic talent—your beautiful watercolor paintings make the book extra special. I love the personal touch, and enjoyed collaborating with you on the artwork.

To Grandpa Nate, if there's one thing you bring, it's gravitas. Thank you for always encouraging me and being there to chat when I need advice. Gail, thank you for helping with recipe testing. What a privilege it was to grow up around the corner from you both.

To Grandpa Michael, I know you'll eat anything and everything, but I still always appreciate when you like the things I make.

To Grandpa Lenny, we miss you so much. Thank you for always being so excited about my cooking endeavors and for passing on lots of wisdom about meat.

To Aunt Rachel, you make some of the most delicious home-cooked meals I've ever had. Thanks for always sharing your tips and tricks with me. You've made me a much better cook.

To Erica Rose, thank you for being so helpful with recipe testing and for being my original blog proofreader.

Love to all my cousins, aunts, and uncles: Uncle David, Michael, Jenny, and Ben; Uncle Andy, Uncle Pete, Bella, Samuel, Cora, Nathaniel, Josephine, Beth, Jason and Lindsay; Aunt Laura, Bobby and Daniel, Aunt Melinda, Aunt Jessica, and Max.

Special thanks to Anne Edelstein for connecting me with Laura and giving me advice in the book world.

To Catherine, David, Uncle Stu, and all the Dunns, it's rare to have second cousins feel so close, and I feel lucky to have you.

To Kaela Marcus Kurn, Maia Matheny, and Maeve Day, thanks for more than a decade of friendship and the brown butter fiasco. Kaela, you know what you did in May 2013.

To Odeya Rosenband, thank you for tasting nearly every recipe at school, doing the dishes after our dinners, and for your frequent consultations, even when you were halfway around the world.

To Maddie Aptman, thanks for humbling me in the best ways possible, for going to my silly influencer events, and for being my honeymoon partner. And to your family—Eileen, Lowell, Izzy, and Ezra—thank you for being so inclusive and generous in New York and beyond.

To Olivia Weinberg, I love sharing your curiosity about food. I am still waiting for that chocolate cake recipe you promised on the Facebook group.

To Andrea Gómez, I'm glad one of us still majored in food science! I'm so happy we are neighbors in the real world after being roommates in school.

To Kailey O'Donnell, Megan, and all the Badagliaccas, thank you for sharing your beautiful Italian culture with me.

To Dylan Brenner, thanks for sharing your enthusiasm for food (and matcha) with me and for always being down for adventures in the city.

Sammi Landsman, even though you tried to kill Hazel, you'll always be babushka chic.

Kayla Bouazouni, thank you for being such a good friend to my sister, my fellow steak lover, and the perfect Parisian tour guide.

To everyone in the Clamiglia—Natalie, Claire, Mike, Jacob, Miranda, Hayley, Audrey, Xavier, Charlie, John, and Colton, thanks for always being a comedic relief and an eager source of taste testers at school.

Thank you to Millie Hillman for your delicious chickpeas and morsels of wisdom. You saw the vision early on.

Thanks to Jenn Segal for the original book advice :)

Thank you to the Mom Squad: Lynne Matheny for being such a helpful consultant with the pantry staples; Karen Jacob for being the most professional recipe tester and thorough proofreader; and Maya Godofsky for the constructive comments.

Thanks to Jenn Collins for recipe testing.

Thank you to Jake Cohen for the advice whenever this project seemed overwhelming.

To Jake and Eli Rallo and the entire family, thanks for sharing your love and enthusiasm for good wine and food with me.

Major thank you to Matt Casler, Amelia Chikota, Amy Eng, Greta Gooding, Monte Longoria, Lei Rabeje, Abby Reing, and Blake Röwe for being my trusted extra sets of eyes at the very end. Your help let me sleep much better at night!

Special thanks to Aurora Cavallo and the rest of the Cavallo family—your hospitality and passion for food is inspiring.

Also thank you to Smeg USA for contributing an amazing oven and refrigerator to the project.

Nora Barak, Margaret Chan, Jack Connors, Adam Faletsky, Asher Faletsky-Röwe, Zoë Fleishaker, Gaby Furman, Olivia Gee, Isaac Gershberg, Paris Ghazi, Haani Jetha, Sama Joshi, Claire Meakem, Liam Motley, Jacob Novozhenets, Lindsey Sexton, Shapiro Sisters, Rae Specht, Thomas Tedesco, Vicenç Vilà-Coury, Maya Voelkel, Audrey Zantzinger, Max Zavidow, Julia Zimmerman—all the time we've spent together and the conversations we've had during this process have been an amazing outlet.

Love to ALL my internet and foodie friends including:

Matt Adlard, Shreya Ahluwalia, Edgar Castrejón, Hailee Catalano, Mariam Daud, August DeWindt, Nick DiGiovanni, Justine Doiron, Emily Fedner, Jack Goldburg, Ashley Hamilton, Meredith Hayden, Zaynab Issa, Jon Kung, Nasim Lahbichi, Hank Laporte, Luca Manfé, Emily Mariko, Hallie Meyer, Joanne Molinaro, Nadia Caterina Munno, Christina Najjar, Alexis Nelson, Claire Parker, Justin Schuble, Violet Witchel. Even though I only interact with some of you online, I feel such a camaraderie doing our silly little things together, and I love seeing how they become the most amazing big serious things.

So much love for my teachers who made a difference during my formative years including:

Ms. Amachi, Ms. Balimtas, Master Coles, Ms. Friis, Sra. Fuentes, Srta. García, Ms. Gleason, Sr. Godínez, Ms. Goldfarb, Dr. Hogewood, Ms. Le, Ms. Lyddane, Sra. Pacheco, Ms. Pagán, Sra. Pomeroy, Ms. Smithson, Ms. Sultan, Sra. Xeron.

To my Cornell professors and faculty including Prof. Aboulhosn, Dr. van Amburgh, Dr. Baraldi, Dr. Bitar, Dr. Brann, Dr. Campbell, Marin Elise Cherry, Dr. Colanzi, Dr. Dedrick, Dr. Lawless, Dr. Litvak, Dr. Loss, Dr. Migiel, Prof. Moss, Dr. Pinet, Dr. Pritts, and Dr. von Wittelsbach—I am so grateful to have explored food science, horticulture, animal science, viticulture and enology, food studies, Spanish, Italian, Jewish studies, photography, and anthropology with you all. I believe you all had a direct role in preparing me to write this book.

To my role models: Ina Garten, Samin Nosrat, Melissa Clark, Padma Lakshmi, Julia Child, and Anthony Bourdain, it is your work that activated me as a child and continues to inspire me now.

Thank you to Samantha Seneviratne: I was blown away by your mastery of food styling. Shooting the cookbook myself was very scary, and you made the first week go by so smoothly. With your expert styling, my recipes looked better than I could have ever imagined.

Laura Manzano, thank you especially for organizing the entire photo shoot in addition to food styling during the second week. I would never have been able to plan when to shop, prep, and execute each recipe in an efficient manner.

To Fatima Khamise, you are one of the most talented cooks and food stylists I have ever worked with. Not only were you an amazing assist to Samantha, I am so grateful that you could lead the additional photo shoot day.

Thank you to Anne Eastman for going so above and beyond for our prop styling. I trust your opinion on anything. If you want me to jump off a cliff, I'll ask how high. Your artistic lens was so helpful with not only the props, but also in creative directing the photography as a whole. Your industry expertise was invaluable in guiding my first shoot, and the continuity of having you with us every day was also critical to our success.

Thanks to Spencer Richards and Jessica Kirkham for assisting Laura and Anne; your work and positive attitudes made us all shine even more.

Thanks also to Chris Galeano for helping with the photography setup. I appreciated getting out of my comfort zone with some of the light setups; it definitely made the photos pop!

Thank you to Morgan Goldstein for keeping me sane in October when we made coffee cake and home fries way too many times, for all your help with Maude, and for making the final stretch so much smoother.

Thanks to my manager, Alix Frank, and Mack Davey for helping with all things ScheckEats while working on the book. It wasn't always easy to juggle everything and I could not have done it without you guys.

Melissa Lotfy, your book design exceeded my best expectations. It was a dream come true to see my Word document take shape and actually look like a book.

Thank you to my agents, Laura Nolan and Jon Michael Darga, for helping me through the entire book process—you are the ones who turned my concept into my life! Thank you for always being my advocates.

To my editor, Stephanie Fletcher, thanks for seeing my vision for this book so clearly. Your calm energy has helped make this process almost entirely a joy, when it could easily have been extremely stressful. I'm so grateful to have had you in my corner.

208 ACKNOWLEDGMENTS

Universal Conversion Chart

Oven temperature equivalents

250°F = 120°C

275°F = 135°C

300°F = 150°C

325°F = 160°C

350°F = 180°C

375°F = 190°C

400°F = 200°C

425°F = 220°C

450°F = 230°C

475°F = 240°C

500°F = 260°C

Measurement equivalents

Measurements should always be level unless directed otherwise.

⅛ teaspoon = 0.5 mL

¼ teaspoon = 1 mL

½ teaspoon = 2 mL

1 teaspoon = 5 mL

1 tablespoon = 3 teaspoons = ½ fluid ounce = 15 mL

2 tablespoons = ⅛ cup = 1 fluid ounce = 30 mL

4 tablespoons = ¼ cup = 2 fluid ounces = 60 mL

5⅓ tablespoons = ⅓ cup = 3 fluid ounces = 80 mL

8 tablespoons = ½ cup = 4 fluid ounces = 120 mL

10⅔ tablespoons = ⅔ cup = 5 fluid ounces = 160 mL

12 tablespoons = ¾ cup = 6 fluid ounces = 180 mL

16 tablespoons = 1 cup = 8 fluid ounces = 240 mL

Recipes by Diet

Note: o = optional

Recipe	Page	Vegan	Vegetarian	Dairy-free	Gluten-free	All Staple Ingredients
Aglio e Olio	79	x	x	x		x
All-Purpose Yogurt Marinade	126		x		x	x
Apple Streusel Muffins	12		x			
Apple Pie Oatmeal	18		x		x	
Apricot-Glazed Chicken	133			x	x	
Apricot Vinaigrette	41	x	x	x	x	x
Aunt Rachel's Infinitely Adaptable Ginger Chicken Soup	143			x	x	
Bakery Coffee Cake	15		x			x
Bakery-Style Chocolate Chip Cookies	192		x			x
Balsamic Vinaigrette (My Way)	40	x	x	x	x	x
Basic Risotto	92		o		x	x
Black Bean Burgers	108		x	x		
Brown Butter Chocolate Chip Cookies	188		x			x
Brown Butter Zucchini	67		x		x	
Brussels Sprouts Slaw	51	x	x	x	o	
Chicken Thighs with Date Butter Sauce	137				x	
Chickpea Salad	48	x	x	x	x	
Coca-Cola Braised Brisket	119			x	o	
Cranberry Carrot Cake	204		x	o		x
Crispy Fried Eggs in Calabrian Chili Butter	4		x	o	x	x
Crispy Roast Sweet Potatoes	57	x	x	x	x	
Crispy Spiced Chickpeas	107	x	x	x	x	x
Cumin Stewed Chickpeas	103	x	x	x	x	
Easy Green Beans	64	x	x	x	x	
Engagement Short Ribs	122			x	o	
Favorite Banana Bread	200		x			

Recipe	Page	Vegan	Vegetarian	Dairy-free	Gluten-free	All Staple Ingredients
Favorite Vanilla Cake or Cupcakes	183		x			
Grandma Karen's Twice Baked Potatoes	62		x		x	
Homemade Granola	11	o	x	o	x	
Homemade Vanilla Extract	178	x	x	x	x	
Honey Lemon Chicken	138					
Internet-Famous Crispy Roast Potatoes	54	x	x	x	x	
Jalapeño Bacon-Wrapped Dates	160			o	x	
Jammy Tomato Toast with Soft Scramble	8		x	o		
Jewish Mother Chicken Soup	141			x	o	
Kale Salad for Dinner	47				x	
Kale Salad with Lemon Vinaigrette	44		x		x	
Leek Risotto	95		o		x	
Leftover Veggie Omelet	7		o		x	
Leftover Veggie Soup	30	x	x	x	x	
Lemon Pepper Broccoli	38		x		x	
Lemon Vinaigrette	41	x	x	x	x	x
Maple Butter Roast Chicken	152				x	
Maple Za'atar Carrots	33	x	x	x	x	x
Mom's Black Beans	100	x	x		x	
Mom's Favorite Marinade	127	x	x	x	o	x
Mom's Lentils	111	x	x	x	x	
Mom's No-Nonsense Chili	96			x	x	
Mom's Roast Chicken	151			x	x	
Mom's Tortilla Soup	27	o	o	o	x	
Mushrooms but Good	68		x		x	
Oatmeal but Not Depressing	17		x		x	x
Orzo Macaroni and Cheese	91		o			
Oven Crispy Tofu	172	x		x	x	
Pappardelle Panna e Funghi	84		x			
Peanut Ginger Dressing	41	o	x	x	o	

Recipe	Page	Vegan	Vegetarian	Dairy-free	Gluten-free	All Staple Ingredients
Peruvian-Inspired Marinade	127	x	x	x	x	
Pesto alla Genovese	81	o	x	o		
Pomegranate-Glazed Salmon with Coconut Rice	164			o	x	
Pomegranate Za'atar Vinaigrette	41	x	x	x	x	x
Pretzel Blondies	198		x			
Real Fettuccine Alfredo	88		x			x
Red Sauce	87	o	x	x		x
Roasted Broccoli and Cauliflower	34	x	x	x	x	
Roasted Parsnips and Carrots	37	x	x	x	x	
Sausage and Peppers Dinner	159			x	x	
Sesame Miso Dressing	41	x	x	x	o	x
Sheet Pan Teriyaki Salmon and Veggies	168			x	o	
Slow-Cooked Ginger Chicken	134			x	o	
"Soy Vay" Roast Chicken	155			x	o	
Spicy Rigatoni alla Vodka	74		x			
Spicy Za'atar Marinade	126		x		x	x
Sweet-and-Spicy Balsamic Vinaigrette	40	o	x	x	o	x
Sweet Chili Miso Brussels Sprouts	52	x	x	x	o	
Sweet Chili Miso Marinade	126	x	x	x	o	x
Sweet Chili Miso Salmon	167			x	o	
Tangy Key Lime Pie with Gingersnap Crust	197		x		o	
Vanilla Cream Cheese Frosting	180		x		x	x
Vanilla Sugar	177	x	x	x	x	
Whipped Cream	195		x			x
You Can Just Eat a Baked Potato	61	x	x	x	x	x
Za'atar Roast Chicken	156				x	

Index

Note: Page references in italics indicate photographs.

Notes

Is Cheese Vegetarian?

1. Pardon, B. & Catry, B. & Boone, R. & Theys, H. & De Bleecker, K. & Dewulf, J. & Deprez, P., (2014) "Characteristics and challenges of the modern Belgian veal industry," Vlaams Diergeneeskundig Tijdschrift 83(4), 155-163. doi: https://doi.org/10.21825/vdt.v83i4.16641

Don't Poison Yourself: Food Safety 101

2. "Chicken and Food Poisoning," CDC, accessed February 23, 2023, https://www.cdc.gov/foodsafety/chicken.html.

Breakfast

3. "Perfluorooctanoic Acid (PFOA), Perfluorooctane Sulfonate (PFOS), and Related Chemicals," American Cancer Society, last modified July 28, 2022, https://www.cancer.org/healthy/cancer-causes/chemicals/teflon-and-perfluorooctanoic-acid-pfoa.html.

4. XiaoZhi Lim, "Tainted Water: The Scientists Tracing Thousands of Fluorinated Chemicals in Our Environment," *Nature* 566 (2019): 26–29, https://www.nature.com/articles/d41586-019-00441-1?utm_medium=affiliate&utm_source=commission_junction&utm_campaign=CONR_PF018_ECOM_GL_PHSS_ALWYS_DEEPLINK&utm_content=textlink&utm_term=PID100064639&CJEVENT=e0c54e4a73fc11ed8027d17e0a82b83.

5. T. H. Begley, K. White, P. Honigfort, M. L. Twaroski, R. Neches, and R. A. Walker, "Perfluorochemicals: Potential Sources of and Migration from Food Packaging," *Food Additives & Contaminants* 22, no. 10 (2005) 1023–1031, https://doi.org/10.108%2652030500183474.

6. Joshua Drobina, "Fumes from Burning Plastic, Welding, and 'Teflon Flu,'" National Poison Control Center, accessed February 23, 2023, https://www.poison.org/articles/fumes-from-burning-plastic-welding-and-teflon-flu-223.

7. Colleen Ford, "How to Care for Stainless Steel Pots and Pans," AMLI Blog, September 30, 2022, https://www.amli.com/blog/how-to-care-for-stainless-steel-pots-and-pans.

Vegetables

8. J. Kenji López-Alt, "The Truth About Cast Iron Pans," Serious Eats, last modified July 7, 2022, https://www.seriouseats.com/the-truth-about-cast-iron.

9. "What Is Cast Iron Seasoning?," Lodge Cast Iron, accessed February 23, 2023, https://www.lodgecastiron.com/cleaning-and-care/cast-iron/science-cast-iron-seasoning.

10. Sheryl Canter, "Chemistry of Cast-Iron Seasoning: A Science-Based How-To," Sheryl's Blog, January 28, 2010, https://sherylcanter.com/wordpress/201%1/a-science-based-technique-for-seasoning-cast-iron/.

11. "Why Does Chopping an Onion Make You Cry?," Library of Congress Everyday Mysteries, last modified December 12, 2021, https://www.loc.gov/everyday-mysteries/food-and-nutrition/item/why-does-chopping-an-onion-make-you-cry/.

12. Maillard is a French name pronounced in American English /my-yahr/ or in the international phonetic alphabet /maɪˈjɑːˌɹiˈækʃən/.

Pastas, Rice, and Beans

13. Amanda R. Kirpitch and Melinda D. Maryniuk, "The 3 R's of Glycemic Index: Recommendations, Research, and the Real World," *Clinical Diabetes* 29, no. 4 (October 1, 2011): 155–159, https://doi.org/10.2337/diaclin.29.4.155.

Proteins

14. "Checking Oven Temperature," Video, America's Test Kitchen, https://www.cooksillustrated.com/videos/144-checking-oven-temperature?extcode=L1BN4BA00.

15. Jo Marshall, "Braising Was Peasant's Way to Tenderize Meat," *Pocono Record*, January 25, 2010, https://www.poconorecord.com/story/lifestyle/food/201%½4/braising-was-peasant-s-way/51727780007/.

Sweets

16. Alissa Hamilton, "Freshly Squeezed: The Truth About Orange Juice in Boxes," Civil Eats, May 6, 2009, https://civileats.com/2009/05/06/freshly-squeezed-the-truth-about-orange-juice-in-boxes/

17. "Cold-Pressed Juicing: The Pros and Cons," Center for Healthy Living, Kaiser Permanente, accessed February 23, 2023, https://thrive.kaiserpermanente.org/care-near-you/southern-california/healthy-balance/ls_tool/cold-pressed-juicing-the-pros-and-cons/.

About the Author

Jeremy Scheck spent high school perfecting his signature cupcakes, making quiches and coffee cake by the dozen at a local bakery, and teaching cooking demonstrations at Williams-Sonoma. As a tenth grader in 2016, he began documenting his favorite recipes on a blog called *The After School Bakery*. In college, Jeremy learned to make fifty gallons of ice cream in the food science lab, how to prune grape vines in the teaching vineyard, the best way to milk a cow in Northern Italy, and why film photography is an art worth preserving. As a sophomore in 2020, he traded blog photos for video and became a TikTok culinary sensation. Jeremy has been featured on *Today*, the *Washington Post*, *Bloomberg*, BBC Radio, *People*, and *Access Hollywood*, among others. Jeremy is a graduate of Cornell University with a double major in Spanish and Italian and significant coursework in food science. He lives in Brooklyn, New York.